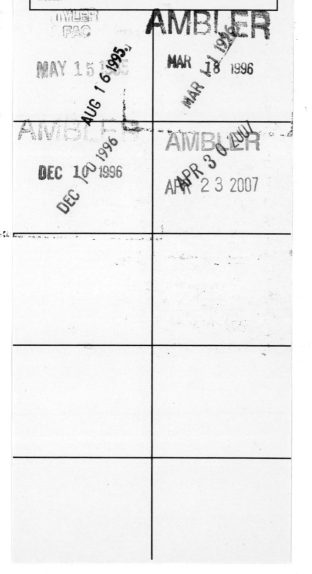
tality of Fact

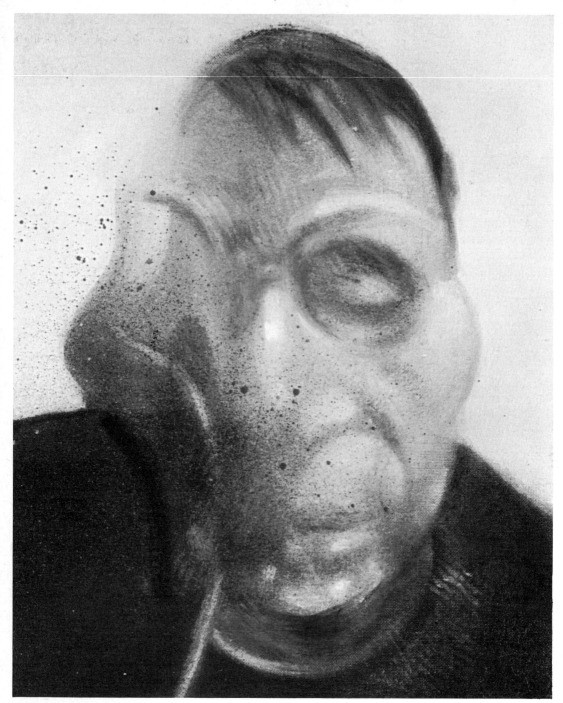

1 (Frontispiece) Detail of centre
panel of *Study for Self-Portrait –
Triptych* 1985–6

# The Brutality of Fact
## Interviews with Francis Bacon

### David Sylvester

*Third enlarged edition*

with 146 illustrations

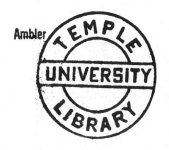
 Thames and Hudson

First published in the USA in 1981 by
Thames and Hudson Inc., 500 Fifth Avenue,
New York, New York 10110
Enlarged edition 1988

Library of Congress Catalog Card Number 87-50197

Previously published in the USA as
*Interviews with Francis Bacon*

Printed in Great Britain by Alden Press, Oxford

Bound in Great Britain

# Contents

Preface 6

Interview 1 8

Interview 2 30

Interview 3 68

Interview 4 108

Interview 5 126

Interview 6 142

Interview 7 156

Interview 8 170

Interview 9 184

Editorial Note 202

Acknowledgments 203

List of Illustrations 204

# Preface

Like the camera, the tape recorder, roughly speaking, cannot lie, and cannot discriminate. Faithfully, it registers every false start, every crossing of purposes, every malformation of syntax and thought, every digression, every unthinking answer or question, every unwitting distortion of fact that results from not having time to remember clearly. None of this matters: the blots and the messes can be edited out. What does matter is the crushing authority of a tape or its transcript. This and only this really is what was said; these are the precise words that were used, more or less precisely, more or less imprecisely. How, then, when it is an interview, do we, having the subject's very words to hand – and rather believing, despite ourselves, that the camera gets nearest to the truth – resist the temptation to treat these words as holy writ, regardless of how imprecise they are? It is a problem that does not trouble the interviewer who eschews mechanical aids and through this discipline leaves himself free to set down not what the subject happened to say but what he meant to say.

I have used tapes for these interviews, and have certainly bowed to their authority in handling Bacon's words. Though making some modifications to clarify syntax – aiming to clarify without tidying up – and now and then altering a word to avoid repetition or too opaque an ambiguity, I have been methodically slavish to Bacon's turns of phrase. There are surely times when his intended meaning could have been brought out more clearly had I stuck less closely to the words in the transcripts, but sticking closely has preserved the very particular rhythms and gestures of his speech, and these, after all, are not the least part of meaning.

At the same time, what is preserved here amounts to no more than about a fifth of the material in the transcripts – out of choice, not because of any arbitrary limitation on length. Furthermore, since the editing has been designed to present Bacon's thought clearly and economically – not to provide some sort of abbreviated record of how the taped sessions happened to develop – the sequence in which things were said has been drastically rearranged. Each of the interviews, apart from the first, has been constructed from transcripts of two or more sessions, and paragraphs in these montages sometimes combine things said on two or three different days quite widely separated in time. In order to prevent the montage from looking like a montage, many of the questions have been recast or simply fabricated. The aim has been to seam together a more concise and coherent argument than ever came about when we were talking, without making it so coherent as to lose the fluid, spontaneous flavour of talk.

As to the problem of whether to insert, as in parliamentary reports, indications of where there was laughter, my conclusion was that, if one does this, one must also logically indicate whether each and every statement was made gravely, laconically, insistently, sarcastically, cautiously, patiently. Perhaps I should, indeed, have presented the text in a form like that of many modern plays, packed with stage directions.

The first edition of this book, published in 1975, contained four interviews, dating from 1962 to 1974; the second edition, published in 1980, added three more, dating from 1975 to 1979; the present edition adds two, dating from 1982 to 1986. The nine printed interviews have between them been based on four different kinds of spoken material: audio recordings made for broadcasting or distribution; filmed recordings made likewise; audio recordings made privately; unrecorded conversations. The editorial note at the back of the book gives precise details of the sources or combinations of sources drawn upon for each interview.

When I take a fresh look at the transcripts of recordings which were the raw material, I come across passages whose omission from the published interviews for the sake of coherence and flow seems a matter for regret. Bacon and I do not intend to do further interviews; but it might be worthwhile for someone – probably not myself – to go through the transcripts one day in search of unpublished material that deserves to be printed, and to have it printed.

*May 1987*

## 1

DS  Have you ever had any desire at all to do an abstract painting?

FB  I've had a desire to do forms, as when I originally did three forms at the base of the Crucifixion. They were influenced by the Picasso things which were done at the end of the 'twenties. And I think there's a whole area there suggested by Picasso, which in a way has been unexplored, of organic form that relates to the human image but is a complete distortion of it.

DS  After that triptych, you started to paint in a more figurative way: was it more out of a positive desire to paint figuratively or more out of a feeling that you couldn't develop that kind of organic form further at that time?

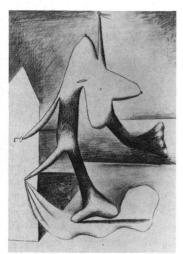

2 PICASSO Charcoal drawing 1927

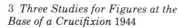
3 *Three Studies for Figures at the Base of a Crucifixion* 1944

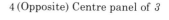
4 (Opposite) Centre panel of *3*

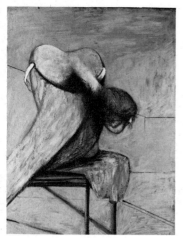

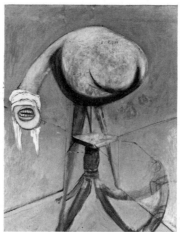

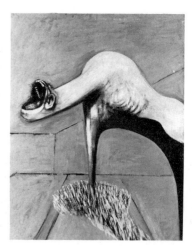

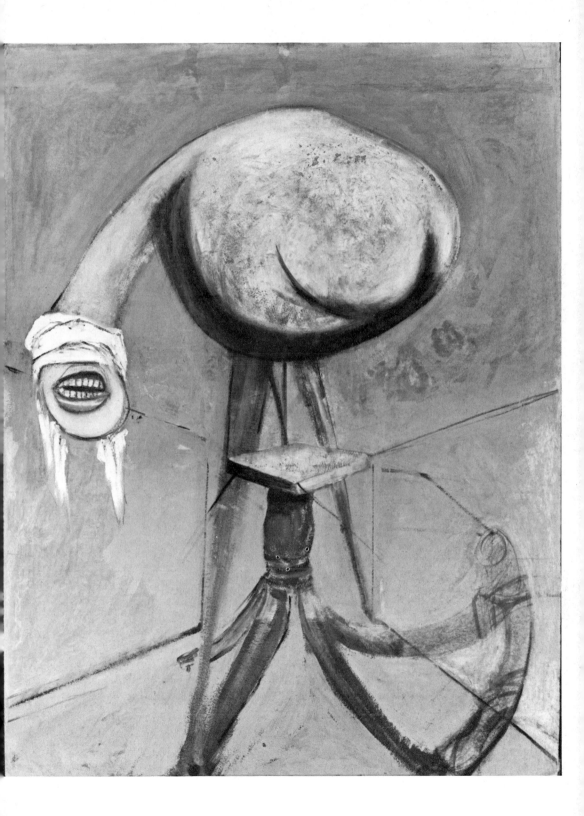

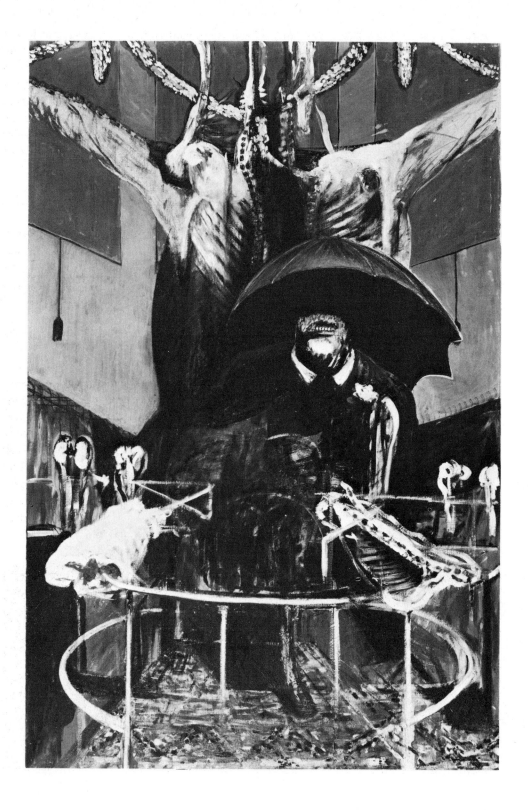

*5 Painting 1946*

FB   Well, one of the pictures I did in 1946, the one like a butcher's shop, came to me as an accident. I was attempting to make a bird alighting on a field. And it may have been bound up in some way with the three forms that had gone before, but suddenly the lines that I'd drawn suggested something totally different, and out of this suggestion arose this picture. I had no intention to do this picture; I never thought of it in that way. It was like one continuous accident mounting on top of another.

DS   Did the bird alighting suggest the umbrella or what?

FB   It suddenly suggested an opening-up into another area of feeling altogether. And then I made these things, I gradually made them. So that I don't think the bird suggested the umbrella; it suddenly suggested this whole image. And I carried it out very quickly, in about three or four days.

DS   It often happens, does it, this transformation of the image in the course of working?

FB   It does, but now I always hope it will arrive more positively. Now I feel that I want to do very, very specific objects, though made out of something which is completely irrational from the point of view of being an illustration. I want to do very specific things like portraits, and they will be portraits of the people, but, when you come to analyze them, you just won't know – or it would be very hard to see – how the image is made up at all. And this is why in a way it is very wearing, because it is really a complete accident.

*6 Three Studies for Portrait of Henrietta Moraes 1963*

DS   An accident in what sense?

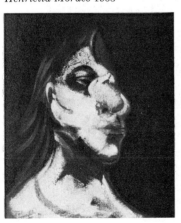 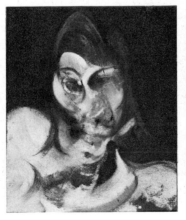 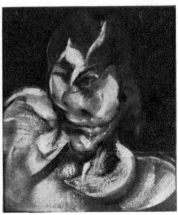

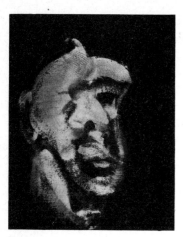

7 *Head I* 1961

FB  Because I don't know how the form can be made. For instance, the other day I painted a head of somebody, and what made the sockets of the eyes, the nose, the mouth were, when you analyzed them, just forms which had nothing to do with eyes, nose or mouth; but the paint moving from one contour into another made a likeness of this person I was trying to paint. I stopped; I thought for a moment I'd got something much nearer to what I want. Then the next day I tried to take it further and tried to make it more poignant, more near, and I lost the image completely. Because this image is a kind of tightrope walk between what is called figurative painting and abstraction. It will go right out from abstraction but will really have nothing to do with it. It's an attempt to bring the figurative thing up onto the nervous system more violently and more poignantly.

DS  In those early paintings you've mentioned, there's a strong red or orange ground, but then the painting became altogether more tonal and for about ten years there were none of those large areas of violent colour.

FB  So far as I can remember, I had a feeling that I could make these images much more poignant in the darkness and without colour.

DS  And can you remember what made you start using strong colour again?

FB  I suppose just getting bored.

DS  Also, when the paintings got darker, the forms became less defined, more smudged.

FB  Well, you can lose the form more easily in darkness, can't you?

DS  Now, in some of your most recent paintings you've both been using strong background colours and gone back to the precise and sculptural sort of forms of that early triptych (*3*) – especially in the right-hand canvas of the new *Crucifixion* triptych. Do you have a general desire now to make the form more clear and precise?

FB  Oh yes, the clearer and more precise the better. Of course, how to be clear and precise is a terribly difficult thing now. And I think that's the problem for all painters now, or at any rate painters who are absorbed in a subject or in a figurative thing. They just want to make it more and more precise; but of a very ambiguous precision.

DS   In painting this *Crucifixion*, did you have the three canvases up simultaneously, or did you work on them quite separately?

FB   I worked on them separately and, gradually, as I finished them, I worked on the three across the room together. It was a thing that I did in about a fortnight, when I was in a bad mood of drinking, and I did it under tremendous hangovers and drink; I sometimes hardly knew what I was doing. And it's one of the only pictures that I've been able to do under drink. I think perhaps the drink helped me to be a bit freer.

DS   Have you been able to do the same in any picture that you've done since?

FB   I haven't. But I think with great effort I'm making myself freer. I mean, you either have to do it through drugs or drink.

DS   Or extreme tiredness?

FB   Extreme tiredness? Possibly. Or will.

DS   The will to lose one's will?

FB   Absolutely. The will to make oneself completely free. Will is the wrong word, because in the end you could call it despair. Because it really comes out of an absolute feeling of it's impossible to do these things, so I might as well just do anything. And out of this anything, one sees what happens.

*8 Three Studies for a Crucifixion*
1962

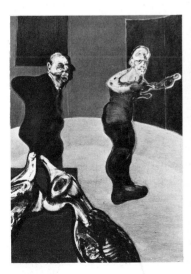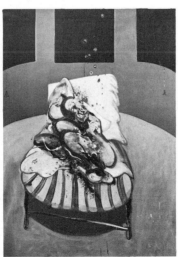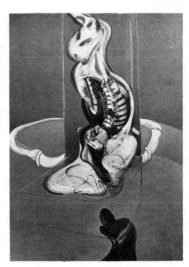

DS   Did the actual placing of the figures change while you were doing this triptych, or did you see them where they are before you started painting?

FB   I did, but they did change continuously. But I did see them, and the figure on the right is something which I have wanted to do for a long time. You know the great Cimabue *Crucifixion*? I always think of that as an image – as a worm crawling down the cross. I did try to make something of the feeling which I've sometimes had from that picture of this image just moving, undulating down the cross.

DS   And of course this is one of a number of existing images you've used.

FB   Yes, they breed other images for me. And of course one's always hoping to renew them.

9 CIMABUE *Crucifixion* 1272–4 (inverted)

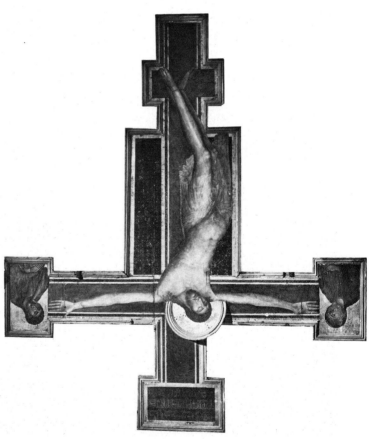

10 (Opposite) Right-hand panel of *8*

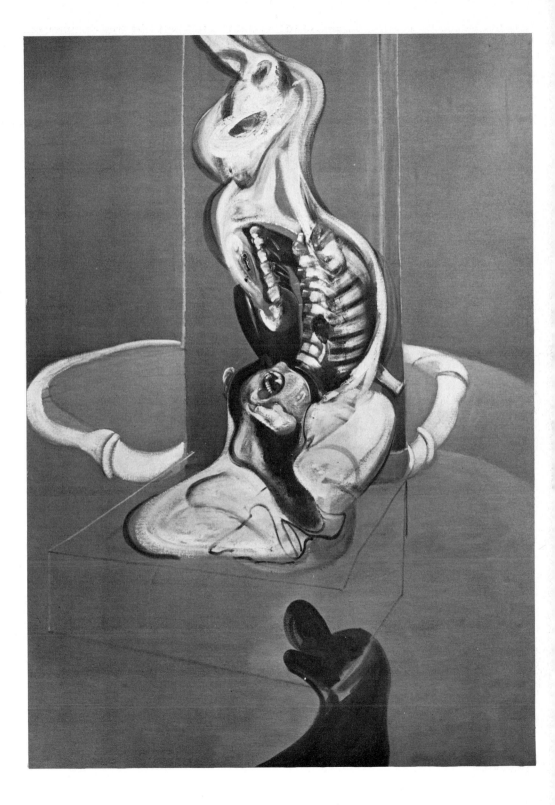

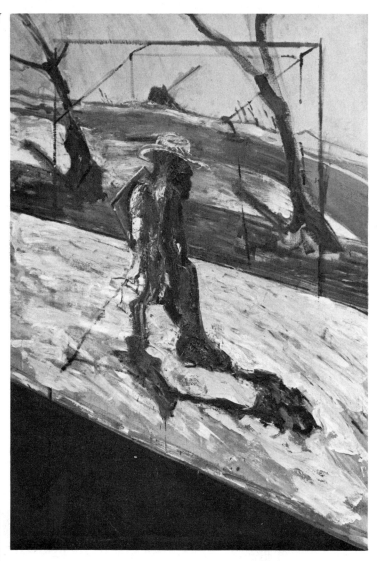

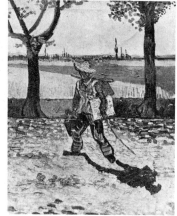

12 VAN GOGH *The Painter on his Way to Work* 1888

DS   And they do get very transformed. But can you generalize about how far you foresee these transformations of existing images before you begin a canvas and how far they happen in the course of painting?

FB   You know in my case all painting – and the older I get, the more it becomes so – is accident. So I foresee it in my mind, I foresee it, and yet I hardly ever carry it out as I foresee it. It transforms itself by the actual paint. I use very large brushes, and in the way I work I don't in fact know very often what the paint will do, and it does many things which are very much better than I could make it do. Is that an accident? Perhaps one could say it's not an accident, because it becomes a selective process which part of this accident one chooses to preserve. One is attempting, of course, to keep the vitality of the accident and yet preserve a continuity.

DS  What is it above all that happens with the paint? Is it the kind of ambiguities that it produces?

FB  And the suggestions. When I was trying in despair the other day to paint that head of a specific person, I used a very big brush and a great deal of paint and I put it on very, very freely, and I simply didn't know in the end what I was doing, and suddenly this thing clicked, and became exactly like this image I was trying to record. But not out of any conscious will, nor was it anything to do with illustrational painting. What has never yet been analyzed is why this particular way of painting is more poignant than illustration. I suppose because it has a life completely of its own. It lives on its own, like the image one's trying to trap; it lives on its own, and therefore transfers the essence of the image more poignantly. So that the artist may be able to open up or rather, should I say, unlock the valves of feeling and therefore return the onlooker to life more violently.

DS  And when you feel that the thing, as you say, has clicked, does this mean that it's given you what you initially wanted or that it's given you what you'd like to have wanted?

FB  One never, of course, I'm afraid, gets that. But there is a possibility that you get through this accidental thing something much more profound than what you really wanted.

DS  When you were talking earlier about this head you were doing the other day, you said that you tried to take it further and lost it. Is this often the reason for your destroying paintings? That's to say, do you tend to destroy paintings early on or do you tend to destroy them precisely when they've been good and you're trying to make them better?

FB  I think I tend to destroy the better paintings, or those that have been better to a certain extent. I try and take them further, and they lose all their qualities, and they lose everything. I think I would say that I tend to destroy all the better paintings.

DS  Can you never get it back once it's gone over the top?

FB  Not now, and less and less. As the way I work is totally, now, accidental, and becomes more and more accidental, and doesn't seem to behave, as it were, unless it is accidental, how can I recreate an accident? It's almost an impossible thing to do.

DS  But you might get another accident on the same canvas.

FB  One might get another accident, but it would never be quite the same. This is the thing that can probably happen only in oil paint, because it is so subtle that one tone, one piece of paint, that moves one thing into another completely changes the implications of the image.

DS  You wouldn't get back what you'd lost, but you might get something else. Why, then, do you tend to destroy rather than work on? Why do you prefer to begin again on another canvas?

FB  Because sometimes it disappears completely and the canvas becomes completely clogged, and there's too much paint on it – just a technical thing, too much paint, and one just can't go on.

DS  Is it because of the particular texture of the paint?

FB  I work between thick and thin paint. Parts of it are very thin and parts of it are very thick. And it just becomes clogged, and then you start to put on illustrational paint.

DS  What makes you do that?

FB  Can you analyze the difference, in fact, between paint which conveys directly and paint which conveys through illustration? This is a very, very difficult problem to put into words. It is something to do with instinct. It's a very, very close and difficult thing to know why some paint comes across directly onto the nervous system and other paint tells you the story in a long diatribe through the brain.

DS  Have you managed to paint any pictures in which you did go on and on and the paint got thick and you still pulled them through?

FB  I have, yes. There was an early one of a head against curtains. It was a small picture, and very, very thick. I worked on that for about four months, and in some curious way it did, I think, perhaps, come through a bit.

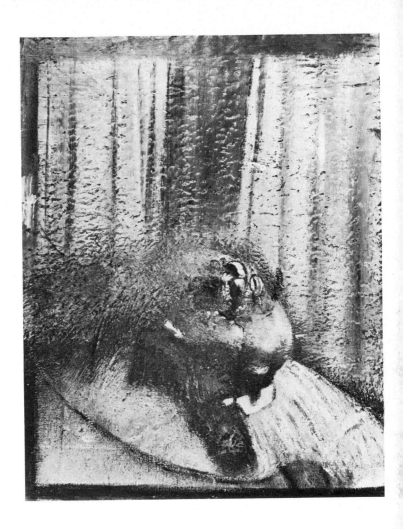

13 *Head II* 1949

DS  But you don't often manage to work on a painting as long as that?

FB  No. But now I find I can work more on paintings. And I hope to be able to have the first instinctive kind of basic thing and then to be able to work on almost directly, as though one was painting a new picture. I've been trying to work that way recently. And I think there are all sorts of possibilities in working directly first and then afterwards bringing this thing that has happened by accident to a much further point by will.

DS  Can you ever turn a painting face to the wall and resume working on it a few weeks or a few months later?

FB  I can't. It has a hypnotic effect upon me, and I can't

leave it alone, so I'm always very glad actually – which is a very bad thing – to try and finish them and get them out of the place as soon as possible.

DS  If people didn't come and take them away from you, I take it, nothing would ever leave the studio; you'd go on till you'd destroyed them all.

FB  I think so, yes.

DS  Have you any positive urge to show them to people? Would it matter to you if they were never seen?

FB  It wouldn't. No. Of course, it's true there are a very, very few people who could help me by their criticism, and I would be very pleased if they liked them at all. But otherwise I don't really care much.

DS  Do you regret the ones you know were good and which you destroyed? Would you like to be able to see them again?

FB  One or two. Yes, a very few I would be very pleased to see again. You see, if they have any quality, they leave memory traces in me which I've never been able to recapture.

DS  Do you ever try to do them again?

FB  I don't. No.

DS  And you never work from sketches or drawings, you never do a rehearsal for the picture?

14 *Pope I* 1951
15 *Pope II* 1951
16 *Pope III* 1951

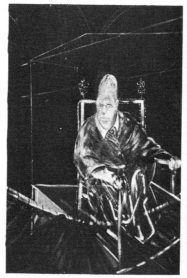 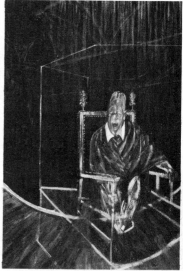

20

FB  I often think I should, but I don't. It's not very helpful in my kind of painting. As the actual texture, colour, the whole way the paint moves, are so accidental, any sketches that I did before could only give a kind of skeleton, possibly, of the way the thing might happen.

DS  And I take it that this also has to do with scale – that to work on a smaller scale for something on a larger scale would be pointless for you.

FB  I think probably.

DS  Actually, your scale is very consistent. Almost everything you paint is pretty well to the same scale. Your smaller paintings are of heads and, when you paint a large painting, it's of a full-length figure: the head in the large painting is the same size as the head in the small one. There are very few cases of a whole figure done in a small painting.

FB  Well, that's my drawback, that's my rigidness.

DS  And the scale is near that of life. So that, when you do a figure, the picture is large, which displeases the collectors.

FB  Yes, but my pictures are not very large compared to so many modern paintings nowadays.

DS  But they seemed to be so ten years ago when everybody was asking you to paint small pictures.

FB  Not any longer. They look rather small pictures now.

DS  You paint a lot in series, of course.

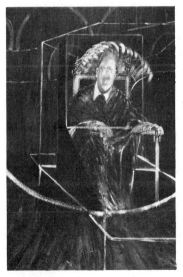

FB  I do. Partly because I see every image all the time in a shifting way and almost in shifting sequences. So that one can take it from more or less what is called ordinary figuration to a very, very far point.

DS  When you're doing a series, do you paint them one after the other or do you work on them concurrently?

FB  I do them one after the other. One suggests the other.

DS  And does a series remain a series for you after you've finished working on it? That's to say, would you like the pictures to be kept together, or is it all the same to you if they get separated?

FB  Ideally, I'd like to paint rooms of pictures with different subject-matter but treated serially. I see rooms full of paintings; they just fall in like slides. I can daydream all day long and see rooms full of paintings. But whether I ever make them really like what drops into my mind, I don't know, because, of course, they fade away. Of course, what in a curious way one's always hoping to do is to paint the one picture which will annihilate all the other ones, to concentrate everything into one painting. But actually in the series one picture reflects on the other continuously and sometimes they're better in series than they are separately because, unfortunately, I've never yet been able to make the one image that sums up all the others. So one image against the other seems to be able to say the thing more.

DS  Most of your paintings have been of single figures or single heads, but in the new *Crucifixion* triptych you've done a composition with several figures *(8)*. Would you like to do that more often?

FB  I find it so difficult to do one figure that that generally seems enough. And, of course, I've got an obsession with doing the one perfect image.

DS  Which would have to be a single figure?

FB  In the complicated stage in which painting is now, the moment there are several figures – at any rate several figures on the same canvas – the story begins to be elaborated. And the moment the story is elaborated, the boredom sets in; the story talks louder than the paint. This is because we are actually in very primitive times once again, and we haven't been able to cancel out the story-telling between one image and another.

DS  And it is true that people have been trying to find a story in the *Crucifixion* triptych. Is there in fact any explanation of the relationship between the figures?

FB  No.

DS  So it's the same thing as when you've painted heads or figures inside a sort of space-frame and it's been supposed that you were picturing someone imprisoned in a glass box.

FB  I use that frame to see the image – for no other reason. I know it's been interpreted as being many other things.

DS  Like when Eichmann was in his glass box and people were saying your paintings had prophesied this image.

FB  I cut down the scale of the canvas by drawing in these

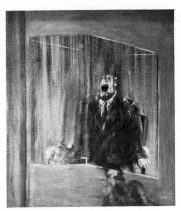

17 *Study for Portrait* 1949

rectangles which concentrate the image down. Just to see it better.

DS   And it never ever had any sort of illustrative intention, not even in that painting of 1949 of a head with microphones?

FB   No, it was just to be able to see the face and the microphones more clearly. I don't think it's a satisfactory device especially; I try to use it as little as possible. But sometimes it seems necessary.

DS   And do the vertical breaks between the canvases of a triptych have the same sort of purpose as those frames within a canvas?

FB   Yes, they do. They isolate one from the other. And they cut off the story between one and the other. It helps to avoid story-telling if the figures are painted on three different canvases. Of course, so many of the greatest paintings have been done with a number of figures on a canvas, and of course every painter longs to do that. But, as the thing's in such a terribly complicated stage now, the story that is already being told between one figure and another begins to cancel out the possibilities of what can be done with the paint on its own. And this is a very great difficulty. But at any moment somebody will come along and be able to put a number of figures on a canvas.

DS   You may not want a story, but you certainly seem to want subjects with a lot of dramatic charge when you choose a theme like the Crucifixion. Can you say what impelled you to do the triptych?

FB   I've always been very moved by pictures about slaughter-houses and meat, and to me they belong very much to the whole thing of the Crucifixion. There've been extraordinary photographs which have been done of animals just being taken up before they were slaughtered; and the smell of death. We don't know, of course, but it appears by these photographs that they're so aware of what is going to happen to them, they do everything to attempt to escape. I think these pictures were very much based on that kind of thing, which to me is very, very near this whole thing of the Crucifixion. I know for religious people, for Christians, the Crucifixion has a totally different significance. But as a non-believer, it was just an act of man's behaviour, a way of behaviour to another.

18 VELASQUEZ *Pope Innocent X*
1650

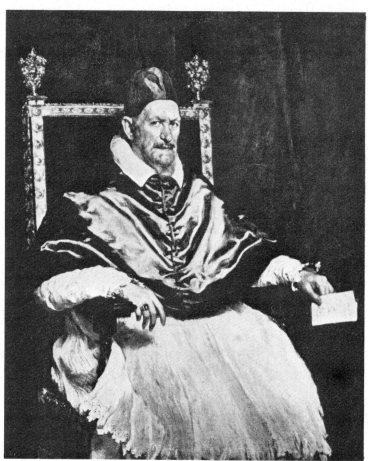

19 *Pope* 1954

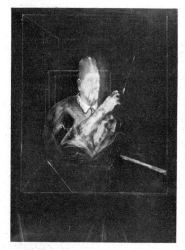

20 *Study of Red Pope (Study from Innocent X)* 1962

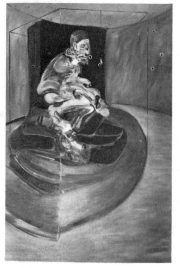

DS  But you do in fact paint other pictures which are connected with religion, because, apart from the Crucifixion, which is a theme you've painted and returned to for thirty years, there are the Popes. Do you know why you constantly paint pictures which touch on religion?

FB  In the Popes it doesn't come from anything to do with religion; it comes from an obsession with the photographs that I know of Velasquez's *Pope Innocent X*.

DS  But why was it you chose the *Pope*?

FB  Because I think it is one of the greatest portraits that have ever been made, and I became obsessed by it. I buy book after book with this illustration in it of the Velasquez *Pope*, because it just haunts me, and it opens up all sorts of feelings and areas of – I was going to say – imagination, even, in me.

24

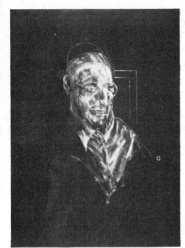

21 *Study for a Head* 1955

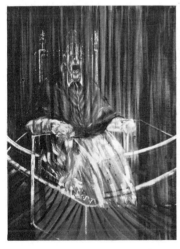

22 *Study after Velasquez's Portrait of Pope Innocent X* 1953

23 *Study after Velasquez* 1950

DS But aren't there other equally great portraits by Velasquez which you might have become obsessed by? Are you sure there's nothing special for you in the fact of its being a Pope?

FB I think it's the magnificent colour of it.

DS But you've also done two or three paintings of a modern Pope, Pius XII, based on photographs, as if the interest in the Velasquez had become transferred onto the Pope himself as a sort of heroic figure.

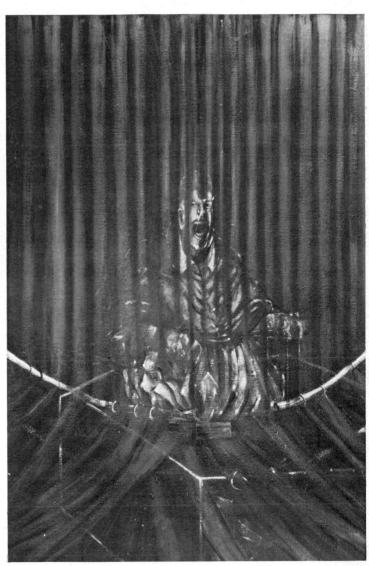

FB   In those magnificent processional photographs when he was being carried through St Peter's. It is true, of course, the Pope is unique. He's put in a unique position by being the Pope, and therefore, like in certain great tragedies, he's as though raised onto a dais on which the grandeur of this image can be displayed to the world.

DS   Since there's the same uniqueness, of course, in the figure of Christ, doesn't it really come back to the idea of the uniqueness and the special situation of the tragic hero? The tragic hero is necessarily somebody who is elevated above other men to begin with.

FB   Well, I'd never thought of it in that way, but when you suggest it to me, I think it may be so.

DS   Because those are the only themes of yours which touch on religion; there are no others. There's the crucified Christ and there's the Pope.

FB   That is true. I think that what you suggest is probably true. It's because they have been forced by circumstances into a unique situation.

DS   And is it the sort of mood implicit in some unique and possibly tragic situation that you want above all?

FB   No. I think, especially as I grow older, I want something much more specific than that. I want a record of an image. And with the record of the image, of course, comes a mood, because you can't make an image without its creating a mood.

DS   A record of an image you've seen in life?

FB   Yes. Of a person, or a thing, but with me it's nearly always a person.

DS   A particular person?

FB   Yes.

DS   But this was less so in the past?

FB   Less so in the past, but now it becomes more and more insistent, only because I think that, by being anchored in that way, there is the possibility of an extraordinary irrational remaking of this positive image that you long to make. And this is the obsession: how like can I make this thing in the most irrational way? So that you're not only remaking the look of the image, you're remaking all the areas

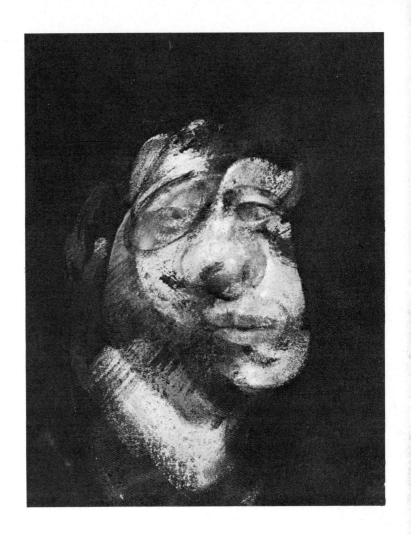

24 Centre panel of *25*

25 *Study for Three Heads* 1962

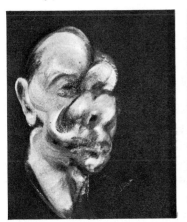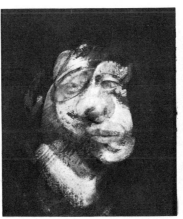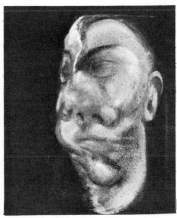

of feeling which you yourself have apprehensions of. You want to open up so many levels of feeling if possible, which can't be done in. . . . It's wrong to say it can't be done in pure illustration, in purely figurative terms, because of course it has been done. It has been done in Velasquez. That is, of course, where Velasquez is so different to Rembrandt, because, oddly enough, if you take the great late self-portraits of Rembrandt, you will find that the whole contour of the face changes time after time; it's a totally different face, although it has what is called a look of Rembrandt, and by this difference it involves you in different areas of feeling. But with Velasquez it's more controlled and, of course, I believe, more miraculous. Because one wants to do this thing of just walking along the edge of the precipice, and in Velasquez it's a very, very extraordinary thing that he has been able to keep it so near to what we call illustration and at the same time so deeply unlock the greatest and deepest things that man can feel. Which makes him such an amazingly mysterious painter. Because one really does believe that Velasquez recorded the court at that time and, when one looks at his pictures, one is possibly looking at something which is very, very near to how things looked. Of course the whole thing has become so distorted and pulled-out since then, but I believe that we will come back in a much more arbitrary way to doing something very, very like that – to being as specific as Velasquez was in recording an image. But of course so many things have happened since Velasquez that the situation has become much more involved and much more difficult, for very many reasons. And one of them, of course, which has never actually been worked out, is why photography has altered completely this whole thing of figurative painting, and totally altered it.

DS  In a positive as well as a negative way?

FB  I think in a very positive way. I think that Velasquez believed that he was recording the court at that time and recording certain people at that time; but a really good artist today would be forced to make a game of the same situation. He knows that the recording can be done by film, so that that side of his activity has been taken over by something else and all that he is involved with is making the sensibility open up through the image. Also, I think that man now realizes that he is an accident, that he is a completely futile being, that he has to play out the game without reason. I think that, even when Velasquez was painting, even when

28

Rembrandt was painting, in a peculiar way they were still, whatever their attitude to life, slightly conditioned by certain types of religious possibilities, which man now, you could say, has had completely cancelled out for him. Now, of course, man can only attempt to make something very, very positive by trying to beguile himself for a time by the way he behaves, by prolonging possibly his life by buying a kind of immortality through the doctors. You see, all art has now become completely a game by which man distracts himself; and you may say it has always been like that, but now it's entirely a game. And I think that that is the way things have changed, and what is fascinating now is that it's going to become much more difficult for the artist, because he must really deepen the game to be any good at all. □ □ □

26 *Study for Portrait III (after the life mask of William Blake)* 1955

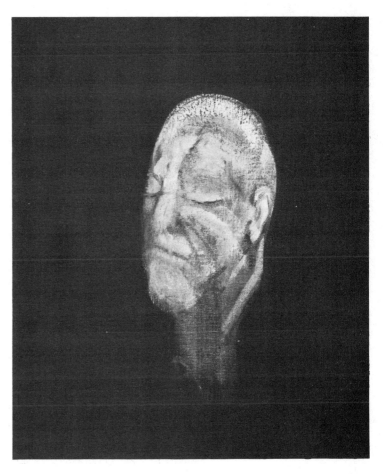

# 2

DS  Can you say why photographs interest you so much?

FB  Well, I think one's sense of appearance is assaulted all
the time by photography and by the film. So that, when one
looks at something, one's not only looking at it directly but
one's also looking at it through the assault that has already
been made on one by photography and film. And 99 per cent
of the time I find that photographs are very much more
interesting than either abstract or figurative painting. I've
always been haunted by them.

DS  Do you know what it is especially that haunts you
about them? Is it their immediacy? Is it the surprising shapes
that happen in them? Is it their texture?

FB  I think it's the slight remove from fact, which returns
me onto the fact more violently. Through the photographic
image I find myself beginning to wander into the image and
unlock what I think of as its reality more than I can by
looking at it. And photographs are not only points of
reference; they're often triggers of ideas.

DS  I suppose that Muybridge's are the photographs you've
made use of most continually.

FB  Well, of course, they were an attempt to make a recording of human motion – a dictionary, in a sense. And the
thing of doing series may possibly have come from looking
at those books of Muybridge with the stages of a movement
shown in separate photographs. I've also always had a book

27, 28 (Opposite) MUYBRIDGE
Sequences of photographs from
*The Human Figure in Motion* 1887

30

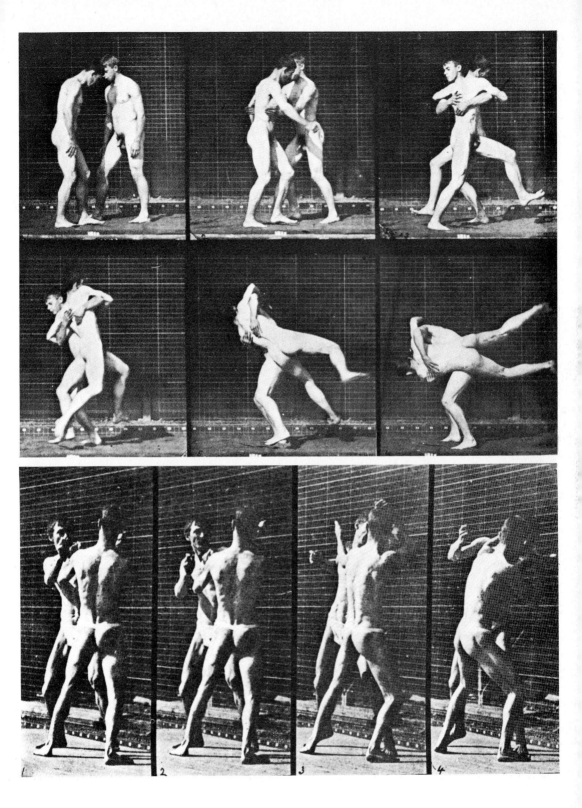

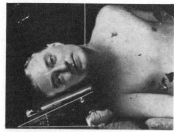

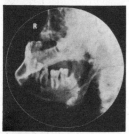

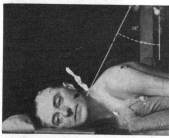

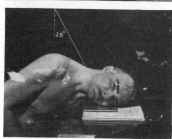

that's influenced me very much called *Positioning in Radiography*, with a lot of photographs showing the positioning of the body for the X-ray photographs to be taken, and also the X-rays themselves.

DS  The influence, though, tends to be oblique – for instance, in that you'll often, while painting, be looking at a photograph of something quite other than the subject you're painting.

FB  I think you've said somewhere that, when you were sitting for a portrait I was trying to do of you, I was always looking at photographs of wild animals.

DS  Yes, I never knew quite how to take that.

FB  Well, one image can be deeply suggestive in relation to another. I had an idea in those days that textures should be very much thicker, and therefore the texture of, for instance, a rhinoceros skin would help me to think about the texture of the human skin.

DS  Of course, you did also use those photographs in a more literal way, in paintings of animals and some landscapes (*53*).

29 (Above) Series of photographs from K.C. CLARK, *Positioning in Radiography* 1929

30 (Right) Photograph from *Positioning in Radiography*

31 (Opposite, above) MUYBRIDGE Page of selected photographs from *The Human Figure in Motion*

32 (Opposite, below) MARIUS MAXWELL Photograph from *Stalking Big Game with a Camera in Equatorial Africa* 1924

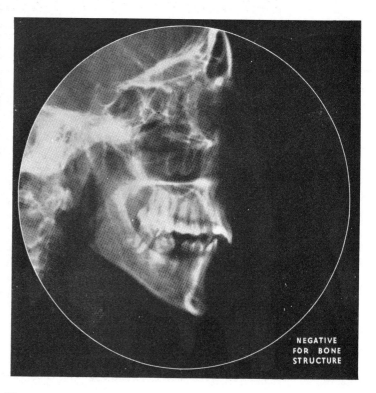

NEGATIVE FOR BONE STRUCTURE

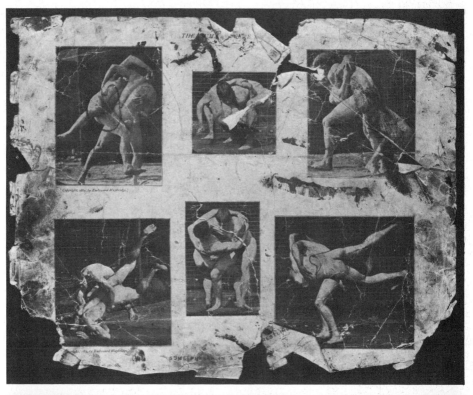

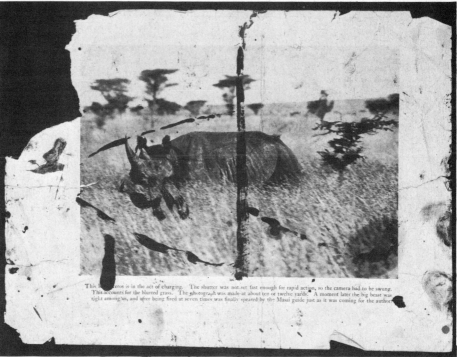

This rhinoceros is in the act of charging. The shutter was not set fast enough for rapid action, so the camera had to be swung. This accounts for the blurred grass. The photograph was made at about ten or twelve yards. A moment later the big beast was right among us, and after being fired at seven times was finally speared by the Masai guide just as it was coming for the author

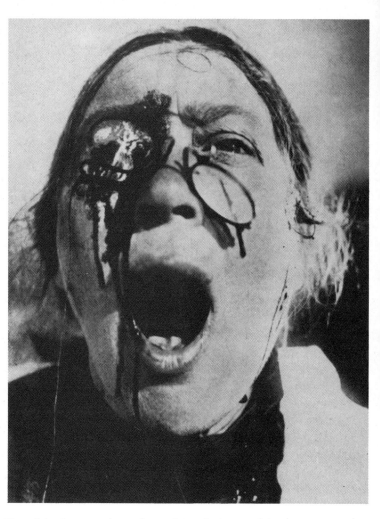

33 EISENSTEIN Still from *The Battleship Potemkin* 1925

But it's interesting that the photographic image you've worked from most of all isn't a scientific or a journalistic one but a very deliberate and famous work of art – the still of the screaming nanny from *Potemkin*.

FB It was a film I saw almost before I started to paint, and it deeply impressed me – I mean the whole film as well as the Odessa Steps sequence and this shot. I did hope at one time to make – it hasn't got any special psychological significance – I did hope one day to make the best painting of the human cry. I was not able to do it and it's much better in the Eisenstein and there it is. I think probably the best human cry in painting was made by Poussin.

DS In *The Massacre of the Innocents*?

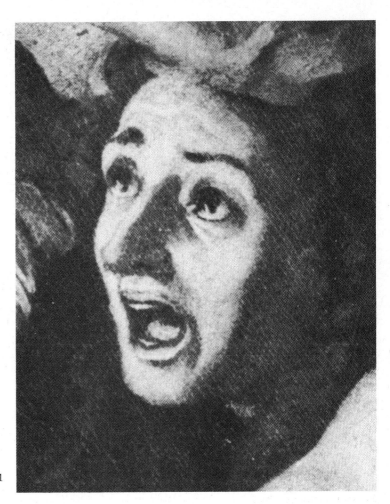

34 Poussin Detail from *The Massacre of the Innocents* 1630–31 (angle altered)

FB Yes, which is at Chantilly. And I remember I was once with a family for about three months living very near there, trying to learn French, and I went a great deal to Chantilly and I remember this picture always made a terrific impression on me. Another thing that made me think about the human cry was a book that I bought when I was very young from a bookshop in Paris, a second-hand book which had beautiful hand-coloured plates of diseases of the mouth, beautiful plates of the mouth open and of the examination of the inside of the mouth; and they fascinated me, and I was obsessed by them. And then I saw – or perhaps I even knew by then – the *Potemkin* film, and I attempted to use the *Potemkin* still as a basis on which I could also use these marvellous illustrations of the human mouth. It never worked out, though.

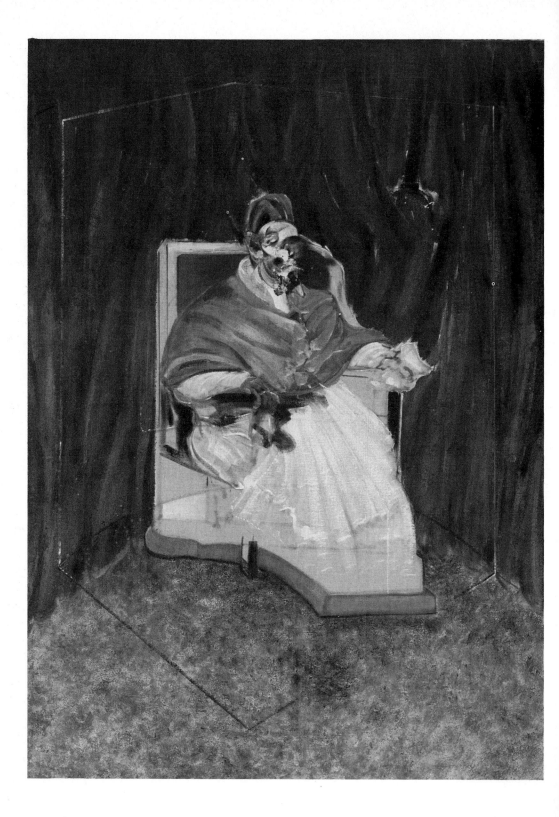

DS You've used the Eisenstein image as a constant basis and you've done the same with the Velasquez *Innocent X*, and entirely through photographs and reproductions of it. And you've worked from reproductions of other old master paintings. Is there a great deal of difference between working from a photograph of a painting and from a photograph of reality?

FB Well, with a painting it's an easier thing to do, because the problem's already been solved. The problem that you're setting up, of course, is another problem. I don't think that any of these things that I've done from other paintings actually have ever worked.

DS Not even any of the versions of the Velasquez *Pope*?

FB I've always thought that this was one of the greatest paintings in the world, and I've used it through obsession. And I've tried very, very unsuccessfully to do certain records of it – distorted records. I regret them, because I think they're very silly.

DS You regret them?

FB Well, I do, because I think that this thing was an absolute thing that was done and nothing more can be done about it.

DS You've stopped painting them now, have you?

FB I have.

DS There are some reproductions of your own paintings among all the photographs lying around the studio. Do you sometimes look at those while you're working?

FB Well, I do very often. For instance, I've been trying to use one image I did around 1952 (*83*) and trying to make this into a mirror so that the figure is crouched before an image of itself. It hasn't come off, but I very often find that I can work from photographs of my own works that have been done years before, and they become very suggestive.

DS I want to ask whether your love of photographs makes you like reproductions as such. I mean, I've always had a suspicion that you're more stimulated by looking at reproductions of Velasquez or Rembrandt than at the originals.

FB Well, of course, it's easier to pick them up in your own room than take the journey to the National Gallery, but I do nevertheless go a great deal to look at them in the National Gallery, because I want to see the colour, for one thing. But, if I'd got Rembrandts here all round the room, I wouldn't go to the National Gallery.

DS  You'd like to have Rembrandts round the room?

FB  I would. There are very few paintings I would like to have, but I would like to have Rembrandts.

DS  Yet, when you finally went to Rome, though you stayed a couple of months, I think, you didn't take the opportunity to see the *Innocent X*.

FB  I didn't. No. It's true to say that at that time I was extremely unhappy emotionally. And, though I loathe churches, I spent most of my time in St Peter's, just wandering around. But I think another thing was probably a fear of seeing the reality of the Velasquez after my tampering with it, seeing this marvellous painting and thinking of the stupid things one had done with it.

DS  So there's clearly nothing in my suspicion. I think I must have supposed that you might prefer photographs to originals because they're less explicit, more suggestive.

FB  Well, my photographs are very damaged by people walking over them and crumpling them and everything else, and this does add other implications to an image of Rembrandt's, for instance, which are not Rembrandt's.

DS  Up to now we've been talking about your working from photographs which were in existence and which you chose. And among them there have been old snapshots which you've used when doing a painting of someone you knew. But in recent years, when you've planned to do a painting of some-body, I believe you've tended to have a set of photographs taken especially.

FB  I have. Even in the case of friends who will come and pose, I've had photographs taken for portraits because I very much prefer working from the photographs than from them. It's true to say I couldn't attempt to do a portrait from photographs of somebody I didn't know. But, if I both know them and have photographs of them, I find it easier to work than actually having their presence in the room. I think that, if I have the presence of the image there, I am not able to drift so freely as I am able to through the photographic image. This may be just my own neurotic sense but

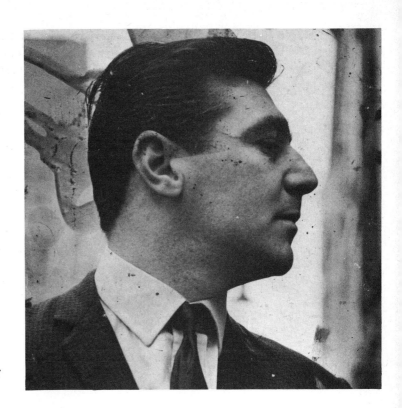

36 JOHN DEAKIN Photograph of
George Dyer

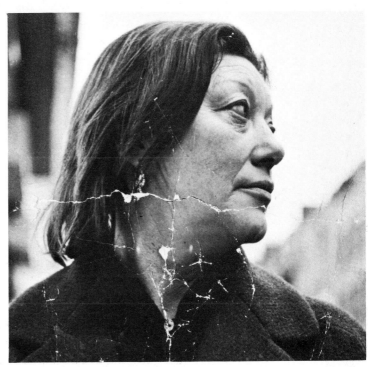

37 JOHN DEAKIN Photograph of
Isabel Rawsthorne

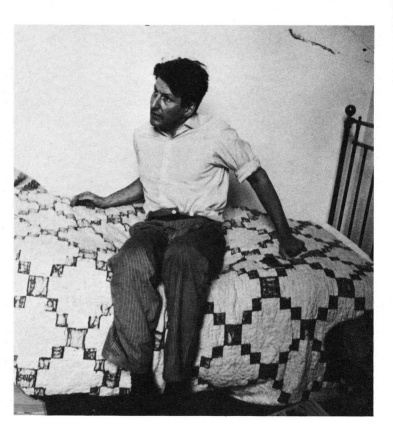

38 JOHN DEAKIN Photograph of
Lucian Freud

I find it less inhibiting to work from them through memory
and their photographs than actually having them seated
there before me.

DS   You prefer to be alone?

FB   Totally alone. With their memory.

DS   Is that because the memory is more interesting or
because the presence is disturbing?

FB   What I want to do is to distort the thing far beyond the
appearance, but in the distortion to bring it back to a
recording of the appearance.

DS   Are you saying that painting is almost a way of bringing
somebody back, that the process of painting is almost like
the process of recalling?

FB   I am saying it. And I think that the methods by which
this is done are so artificial that the model before you, in
my case, inhibits the artificiality by which this thing can be
brought back.

**40**

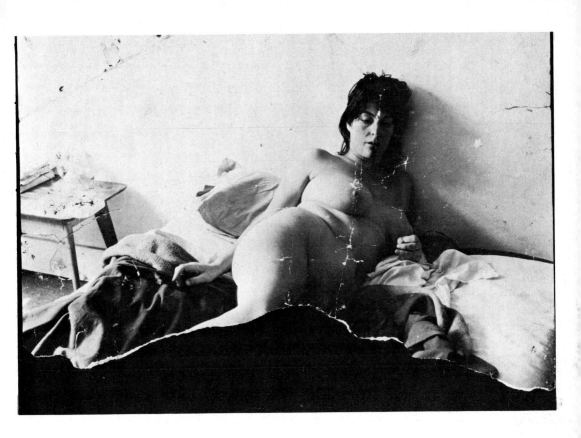

39 JOHN DEAKIN Photograph of
Henrietta Moraes

DS  And what if someone you've already painted many times
from memory and photographs sits for you?

FB  They inhibit me. They inhibit me because, if I like them,
I don't want to practise before them the injury that I do to
them in my work. I would rather practise the injury in
private by which I think I can record the fact of them more
clearly.

DS  In what sense do you conceive it as an injury?

FB  Because people believe – simple people at least – that
the distortions of them are an injury to them – no matter how
much they feel for or how much they like you.

DS  Don't you think their instinct is probably right?

FB  Possibly, possibly. I absolutely understand this. But
tell me, who today has been able to record anything that
comes across to us as a fact without causing deep injury to
the image?

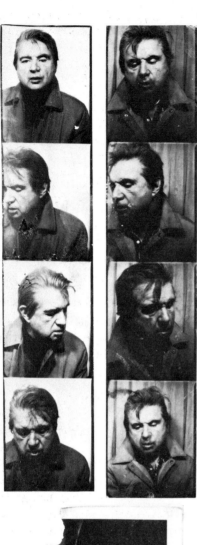
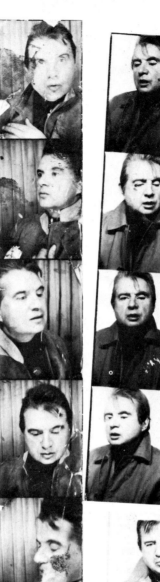
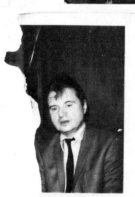
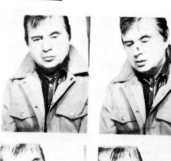
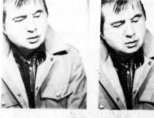

40 Photographs of Bacon taken by himself in automatic booths

DS But do you not think, since you talk about recording different levels of feeling in one image, that, among other things, you may be expressing at one and the same time a love of the person and a hostility towards them – that what you are making may be both a caress and an assault?

FB I think that is too logical. I don't think that's the way things work. I think it goes to a deeper thing: how do I feel I can make this image more immediately real to myself? That's all.

DS Would it not be making it more immediately real to objectify contradictory feelings towards the subject?

FB Well, I think that then you would be going into psychological ways of seeing, and I don't think that most painters do. Although it may be subconsciously involved with what you said, I don't think it is consciously involved at all.

DS Well, of course, if it were conscious it would be disastrous for the work. What I've been trying to suggest is that, when the sitter naïvely supposes that the painter is doing him an injury, he's instinctively recognizing an unconscious desire in the painter to inflict damage.

FB It may be. What you're really saying is what Wilde said: you kill the thing you love. It may be that; I don't know. Whether the distortions which I think sometimes bring the image over more violently are damage is a very questionable idea. I don't think it is damage. You may say it's damaging if you take it on the level of illustration. But not if you take it on the level of what I think of as art. One brings the sensation and the feeling of life over the only way one can. I don't say it's a good way, but one brings it over at the most acute point one can. □ □ □

DS Is it a part of your intention to try and create a tragic art?

FB No. Of course, I think that, if one could find a valid myth today where there was the distance between grandeur and its fall of the tragedies of Aeschylus and Shakespeare, it would be tremendously helpful. But when you're outside a tradition, as every artist is today, one can only want to record one's own feelings about certain situations as closely to one's own nervous system as one possibly can. But in

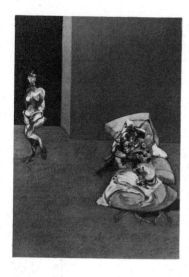
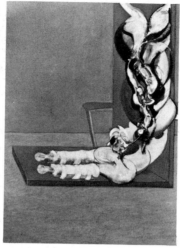
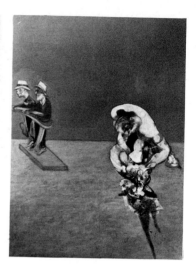

41 *Crucifixion* 1965
43 (Opposite) Centre panel of *41*

42 *Fragment of a Crucifixion* 1950

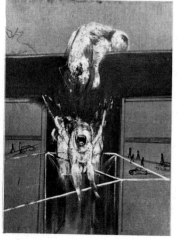

recording these things I may be one of those people who want the distances between what used to be called poverty and riches or between power and the opposite of power.

D S   There is, of course, one great traditional mythological and tragic subject you've painted very often, which is the Crucifixion.

F B   Well, there have been so very many great pictures in European art of the Crucifixion that it's a magnificent armature on which you can hang all types of feeling and sensation. You may say it's a curious thing for a non-religious person to take the Crucifixion, but I don't think that that has anything to do with it. The great Crucifixions that one knows of – one doesn't know whether they were painted by men who had religious beliefs.

D S   But they were painted as part of Christian culture and they were made for believers.

F B   Yes, that is true. It may be unsatisfactory, but I haven't found another subject so far that has been as helpful for covering certain areas of human feeling and behaviour. Perhaps it is only because so many people have worked on this particular theme that it has created this armature – I can't think of a better way of saying it – on which one can operate all types of level of feeling.

D S   Of course, a lot of modern artists in all the media faced with this problem have gone back to the Greek myths. You yourself, in the *Three Studies for Figures at the Base of a*

44

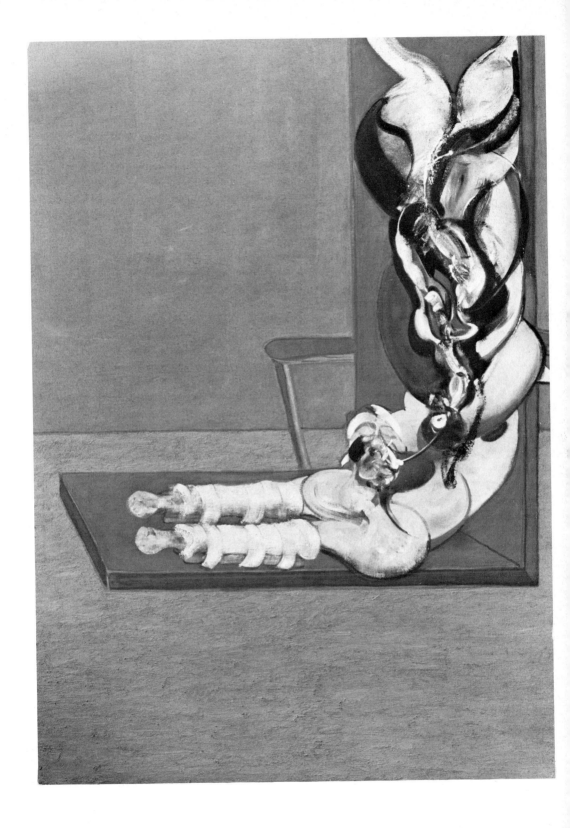

*Crucifixion (3)*, didn't paint the traditional Christian figures at the foot of the Cross, but the Eumenides. Are there other themes from Greek mythology that you've ever thought of using?

F B  Well, I think Greek mythology is even further from us than Christianity. One of the things about the Crucifixion is the very fact that the central figure of Christ is raised into a very pronounced and isolated position, which gives it, from a formal point of view, greater possibilities than having all the different figures placed on the same level. The alteration of level is, from my point of view, very important.

D S  In painting a Crucifixion, do you find you approach the problem in a radically different way from when working on other paintings?

F B  Well, of course, you're working then about your own feelings and sensations, really. You might say it's almost nearer to a self-portrait. You are working on all sorts of very private feelings about behaviour and about the way life is.

D S  One very personal recurrent configuration in your work is the interlocking of Crucifixion imagery with that of the butcher's shop. The connexion with meat must mean a great deal to you.

F B  Well, it does. If you go to some of those great stores, where you just go through those great halls of death, you can see meat and fish and birds and everything else all lying dead there. And, of course, one has got to remember as a painter that there is this great beauty of the colour of meat.

D S  The conjunction of the meat with the Crucifixion seems to happen in two ways – through the presence on the scene of sides of meat and through the transformation of the crucified figure itself into a hanging carcass of meat.

F B  Well, of course, we are meat, we are potential carcasses. If I go into a butcher's shop I always think it's surprising that I wasn't there instead of the animal. But using the meat in that particular way is possibly like the way one might use the spine, because we are constantly seeing images of the human body through X-ray photographs and that obviously does alter the ways by which one can use the body. You must know the beautiful Degas pastel in the National Gallery of a woman sponging her back. And you will find at the very top of the spine that the spine almost comes out of

46

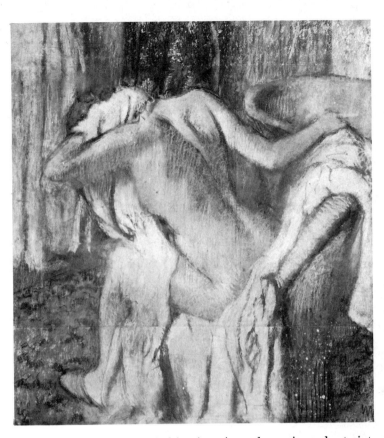

44 DEGAS *After the Bath* 1903

the skin altogether. And this gives it such a grip and a twist that you're more conscious of the vulnerability of the rest of the body than if he had drawn the spine naturally up to the neck. He breaks it so that this thing seems to protrude from the flesh. Now, whether Degas did this purposely or not, it makes it a much greater picture, because you're suddenly conscious of the spine as well as the flesh, which he usually just painted covering the bones. In my case, these things have certainly been influenced by X-ray photographs.

DS   It's clear that much of your obsession with painting meat has to do with matters of form and colour – it's clear from the works themselves. Yet the Crucifixion paintings have surely been among those which have made critics emphasize what they call the element of horror in your work.

FB   Well, they certainly have always emphasized the horror side of it. But I don't feel this particularly in my work. I have never tried to be horrific. One only has to have observed things and know the undercurrents to realize that anything that I have been able to do hasn't stressed that side of life.

When you go into a butcher's shop and see how beautiful meat can be and then you think about it, you can think of the whole horror of life – of one thing living off another. It's like all those stupid things that are said about bull-fighting. Because people will eat meat and then complain about bull-fighting; they will go in and complain about bull-fighting covered with furs and with birds in their hair.

DS  It seems to be quite widely felt of the paintings of men alone in rooms that there's a sense of claustrophobia and unease about them that's rather horrific. Are you aware of that unease?

FB  I'm not aware of it. But most of those pictures were done of somebody who was always in a state of unease, and whether that has been conveyed through these pictures I don't know. But I suppose, in attempting to trap this image, that, as this man was very neurotic and almost hysterical, this may possibly have come across in the paintings. I've always hoped to put over things as directly and rawly as I possibly can, and perhaps, if a thing comes across directly, people feel that that is horrific. Because, if you say something very directly to somebody, they're sometimes offended, although it is a fact. Because people tend to be offended by facts, or what used to be called truth.

DS  On the other hand, it's not altogether stupid to attribute an obsession with horror to an artist who has done so many paintings of the human scream.

FB  You could say that a scream is a horrific image; in fact, I wanted to paint the scream more than the horror. I think, if I had really thought about what causes somebody to scream, it would have made the scream that I tried to paint more successful. Because I should in a sense have been more conscious of the horror that produced the scream. In fact they were too abstract.

DS  They were too purely visual?

FB  I think so. Yes.

DS  The open mouths – are they always meant to be a scream?

FB  Most of them, but not all. You know how the mouth changes shape. I've always been very moved by the movements of the mouth and the shape of the mouth and the teeth. People say that these have all sorts of sexual implications, and I was always very obsessed by the actual appearance of

45 (Opposite) *Study for Figure IV*
1956–7

**48**

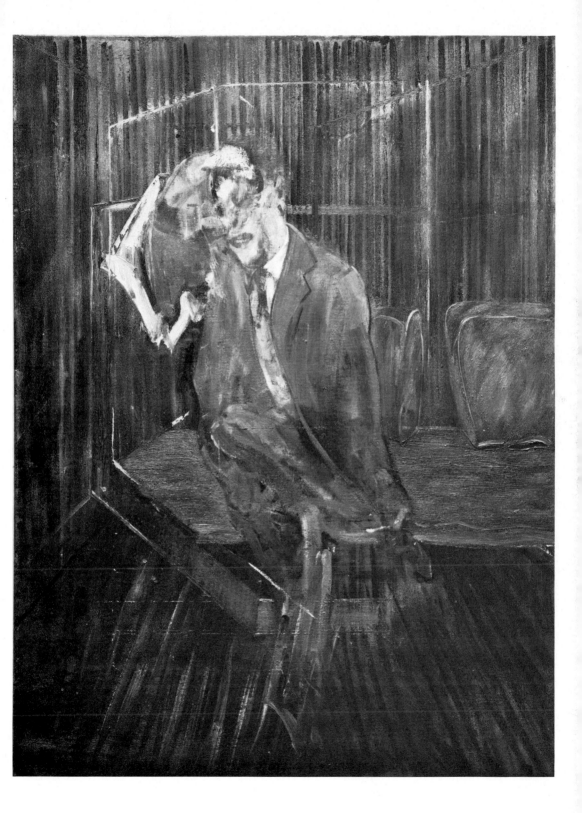

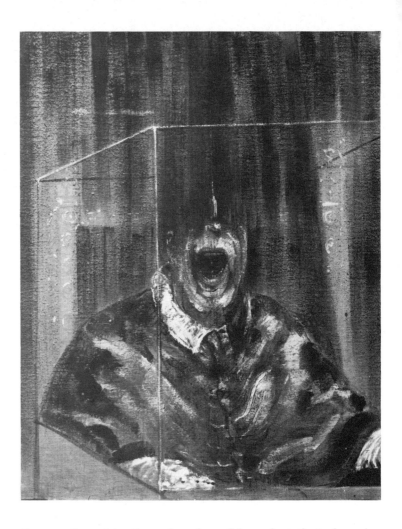

46 *Head VI* 1949

the mouth and teeth, and perhaps I have lost that obsession now, but it was a very strong thing at one time. I like, you may say, the glitter and colour that comes from the mouth, and I've always hoped in a sense to be able to paint the mouth like Monet painted a sunset.

DS  So you might well have been interested in painting open mouths and teeth even if you hadn't been painting the scream?

FB  I think I might. And I've always wanted and never succeeded in painting the smile. □ □ □

DS  You once wrote of painting as being a game of chance. When you go gaming, you play roulette rather than chemmy?

FB   Well, generally, yes.

DS   Because you like the impersonality of it?

FB   I like the impersonality. I hate the personality that chemmy players put on between one another, and so I like the completely impersonal thing of roulette. Also it just happens that I have been luckier at roulette than I have at chemmy. I feel that now my luck has completely deserted me as a gambler, for the present time. Luck's a funny thing; it runs in long patches, and sometimes one runs into a long patch of very good luck. When I was never able to earn any money from my work, I was able sometimes in casinos to make money which altered my life for a time, and I was able to live on it and live in a way that I would never have been able to if I had been earning it. But now I seem to have run out of that patch. I remember when I lived once for a long time in Monte Carlo and I became very obsessed by the casino and I spent whole days there – and there you could go in at ten o'clock in the morning and needn't come out until about four o'clock the following morning – and at that time, which was a good many years ago, I had very little money, and I did sometimes have very lucky wins. I used to think that I heard the croupier calling out the winning number at roulette before the ball had fallen into the socket, and I used to go from table to table. And I remember one afternoon I went in there, and I was playing on three different tables, and I heard these echoes. And I was playing rather small stakes, but at the end of that afternoon chance had been very much on my side and I ended up with about sixteen hundred pounds, which was a lot of money for me then. Well, I immediately took a villa, and I stocked it with drink and all the food that I could buy in, but this chance didn't last very long, because in about ten days' time I could hardly buy my fare back to London from Monte Carlo. But it was a marvellous ten days and I had an enormous number of friends.

DS   It's often said that people gamble in order to lose, and I feel that my own gambling was done in order to lose. Does this apply in your case or do you feel you actually want to win?

FB   I feel I want to win, but then I feel exactly the same thing in painting. I feel I want to win even if I always lose.

DS   When you have a good win, which means more to you: the feeling that the gods are on your side – to use a phrase you've used about chance in painting – or the advantages you get out of it in good living?

FB   I think the advantages I can get out of it.

DS   You like to live well?

FB   I live in, you may say, a gilded squalor. I would hate always to what is called live in luxurious places. But I like, when I want to, to be able to go to them and to live that kind of life.

DS   What is it you like about, say, staying in good hotels?

FB   I like comfort and I like being able to have service easily laid on. I don't live at all that way myself, as you know. But I terribly like, when I go to those places, for it to be very easy to get things done for you that you want, that money buys for you.

DS   Is it the easiness of it or the idea of luxury itself that attracts you?

FB   I think it's the ease. But then, if we go on to luxury, luxury obviously alters people. I mean, one knows that people who can live in luxury and do everything they want generally become desperately bored. And they plan all sorts of little devices and expeditions by which to relieve their boredom. I remember once in the Ritz going up with a rich man who happened to be in the lift, and he'd been in Soho shopping to buy some peas and new potatoes, and the bag burst, and it all fell on the floor of the lift presumably taking him up to his room where I imagine he had a little oil stove where he was able to cook the peas and potatoes. Well, that is luxury for a rich man.

DS   Quite. You were saying that for the moment you've exhausted your luck as a gambler. What about luck in your work?

FB   I think that accident, which I would call luck, is one of the most important and fertile aspects of it, because, if anything works for me, I feel it is nothing I have made myself, but something which chance has been able to give me. But it's true to say that over a great many years I have been thinking about chance and about the possibilities of using what chance can give, and I never know how much it is pure chance and how much it is manipulation of it.

DS   You probably find that you get better at manipulating it.

FB One possibly gets better at manipulating the marks that have been made by chance, which are the marks that one made quite outside reason. As one conditions oneself by time and by working to what happens, one becomes more alive to what the accident has proposed for one. And, in my case, I feel that anything I've ever liked at all has been the result of an accident on which I have been able to work. Because it has given me a disorientated vision of a fact I was attempting to trap. And I could then begin to elaborate, and try and make something out of a thing which was non-illustrational.

DS I can think of three ways in which an accident might happen. One would be when you were exasperated with what you had done and either with a cloth or with a brush freely scrubbed over it. A second would be when you painted impatiently and made marks across the form in annoyance. A third might be when you painted absent-mindedly, when your attention was wandering.

FB Or when you were drunk. Well, of course, all three, or all four, may work; they may or may not. They generally don't, of course.

DS In what other ways would an accident happen, or are those more or less the sorts of ways?

FB I would say that those were the ways. But I think that you can make, very much as in abstract painting, involuntary marks on the canvas which may suggest much deeper ways by which you can trap the fact you are obsessed by. If anything ever does work in my case, it works from that moment

47 *Three Studies for Portrait of Lucian Freud* 1965

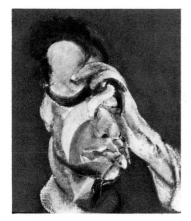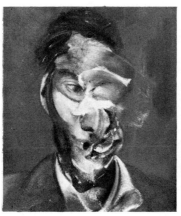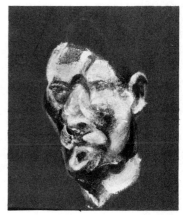

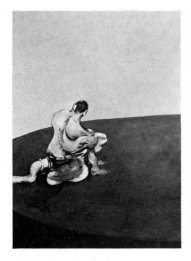 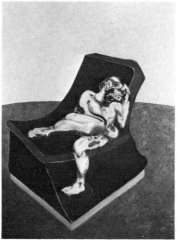 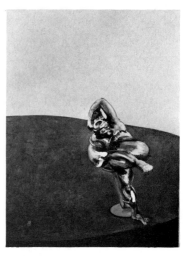

48 *Three Figures in a Room* 1964

when consciously I don't know what I'm doing. I've often found that, if I have tried to follow the image more exactly, in the sense of its being more illustrational, and it has become extremely banal, and then out of sheer exasperation and hopelessness I've completely destroyed it by not knowing at all the marks I was making within the image – suddenly I have found that the thing comes nearer to the way that my visual instincts feel about the image I am trying to trap. It's really a question in my case of being able to set a trap with which one would be able to catch the fact at its most living point.

DS   What are you thinking about at the time? How do you suspend the operation of conscious decision?

FB   At that moment I'm thinking of nothing but how hopeless and impossible this thing is to achieve. And by making these marks without knowing how they will behave, suddenly there comes something which your instinct seizes on as being for a moment the thing which you could begin to develop.

DS   How much does it help to drink when you're painting?

FB   This is a difficult thing to say. I haven't done many things when I have had a lot to drink but I have done one or two. I did the *Crucifixion* in 1962 (8) when I was on drink for about a fortnight. Sometimes it loosens you, but again I think it also dulls other areas. It leaves you freer, but on the other hand it dulls your final judgement of what you hold. I don't actually believe that drink and drugs help me. They may help other people, but they don't really help me.

49 (Opposite) Left-hand panel of *48*

54

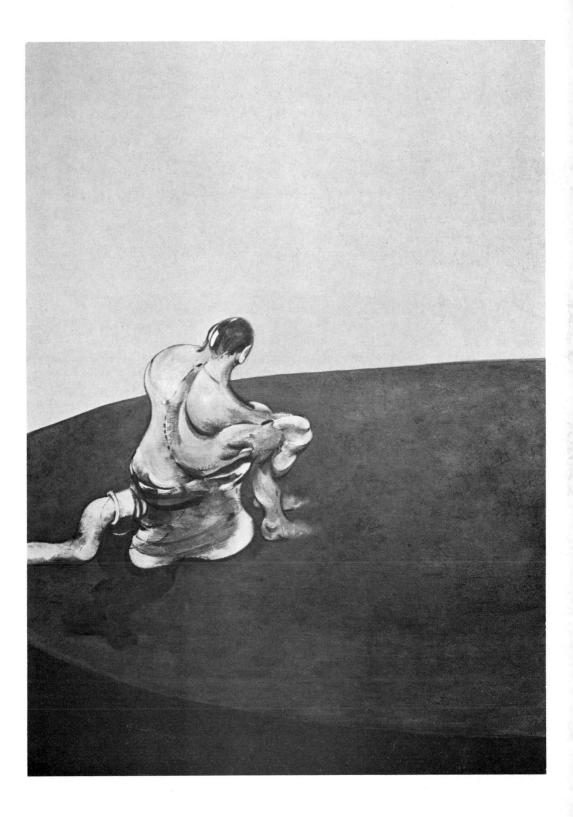

DS   In other words, although you talk about the importance of chance, you really don't want to lose a certain clarity. You don't want to leave too much to chance, do you?

FB   I want a very ordered image but I want it to come about by chance.

DS   But you're sufficiently puritanical not to want to make the chance come too easily.

FB   I would like things to come easily, but you can't order chance. This is the thing. Because if you could, you would only be imposing another type of illustration.

DS   Are you aware of the moment when you find that you are becoming free and the thing is taking you over?

FB   Well, very often the involuntary marks are much more deeply suggestive than others, and those are the moments when you feel that anything can happen.

DS   You feel it while you're making those marks?

FB   No, the marks are made, and you survey the thing like you would a sort of graph. And you see within this graph the possibilities of all types of fact being planted. This is a difficult thing; I'm expressing it badly. But you see, for instance, if you think of a portrait, you maybe at one time have put the mouth somewhere, but you suddenly see through this graph that the mouth could go right across the face. And in a way you would love to be able in a portrait to make a Sahara of the appearance – to make it so like, yet seeming to have the distances of the Sahara.

DS   It's a matter of reconciling opposites, I suppose – of making the thing be contradictory things at once.

FB   Isn't it that one wants a thing to be as factual as possible and at the same time as deeply suggestive or deeply unlocking of areas of sensation other than simple illustration of the object that you set out to do? Isn't that what all art is about?

DS   Could you try and define the difference between an illustrational and a non-illustrational form?

FB   Well, I think that the difference is that an illustrational form tells you through the intelligence immediately what the form is about, whereas a non-illustrational form works first upon sensation and then slowly leaks back into the fact. Now why this should be, we don't know. This may have to do

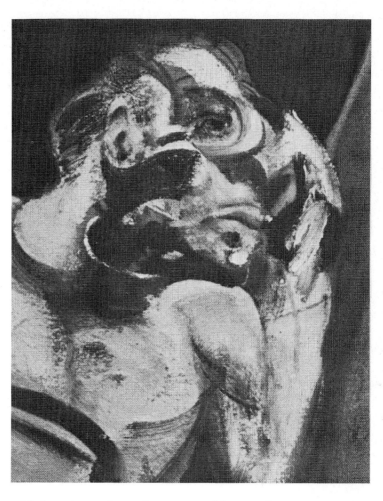

50 Detail from centre panel of *48*

with how facts themselves are ambiguous, how appearances are ambiguous, and therefore this way of recording form is nearer to the fact by its ambiguity of recording.

DS When you get a photograph taken with a high-speed camera that produces an entirely unexpected effect which is highly ambiguous and exciting, because the image is the thing and it isn't, or because it's surprising that this shape is the thing: now, is that illustration?

FB I think it is. I think it is a diverted illustration. I think the difference from direct recording through the camera is that as an artist you have to, in a sense, set a trap by which you hope to trap this living fact alive. How well can you set the trap? Where and at what moment will it click? And there's another thing, that has to do with texture. I think the texture of a painting seems to be more immediate than

57

the texture of a photograph, because the texture of a photograph seems to go through an illustrational process onto the nervous system, whereas the texture of a painting seems to come immediately onto the nervous system. It's terribly like, for instance. ... Supposing you were to think of great ancient Egyptian things made of bubble gum, supposing you were to think of the Sphinx made of bubble gum, would it have had the same effect upon the sensibility over the centuries if you could pick it up gently and lift it?

DS  You're giving this as an example of the effect of a great work's depending on the mysterious way in which the image combines with the material that it's made of?

FB  I think it has to do with endurance. I think that you could have a marvellous image made of something which will disappear in a few hours, but I think that the potency of the image is created partly by the possibility of its enduring. And, of course, images accumulate sensation around themselves the longer they endure.

DS  The thing that's difficult to understand is how it is that marks of the brush and the movement of paint on canvas can speak so directly to us.

FB  Well, if you think of the great Rembrandt self-portrait in Aix-en-Provence, for instance, and if you analyze it, you will see that there are hardly any sockets to the eyes, that it is almost completely anti-illustrational. I think that the mystery of fact is conveyed by an image being made out of non-rational marks. And you can't will this non-rationality of a mark. That is the reason that accident always has to enter into this activity, because the moment you know what to do, you're making just another form of illustration. But what can happen sometimes, as it happened in this Rembrandt self-portrait, is that there is a coagulation of non-representational marks which have led to making up this very great image. Well, of course, only part of this is accidental. Behind all that is Rembrandt's profound sensibility, which was able to hold onto one irrational mark rather than onto another. And abstract expressionism has all been done in Rembrandt's marks. But in Rembrandt it has been done with the added thing that it was an attempt to record a fact and to me therefore must be much more exciting and much more profound. One of the reasons why I don't like abstract painting, or why it doesn't interest me, is that I think painting is a duality, and that abstract painting is an entirely aesthetic thing.

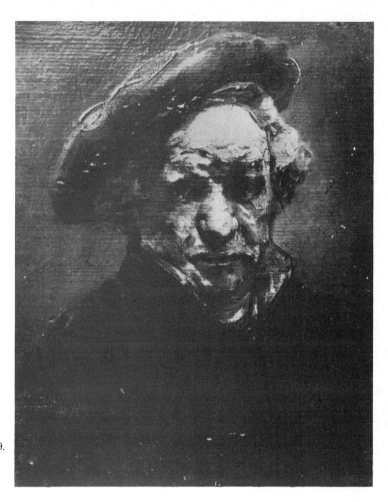

51 REMBRANDT *Self-Portrait* c. 1659. The authenticity of this picture has recently been questioned by certain scholars

It always remains on one level. It is only really interested in the beauty of its patterns or its shapes. We know that most people, especially artists, have large areas of undisciplined emotion, and I think that abstract artists believe that in these marks that they're making they are catching all these sorts of emotions. But I think that, caught in that way, they are too weak to convey anything. I think that great art is deeply ordered. Even if within the order there may be enormously instinctive and accidental things, nevertheless I think that they come out of a desire for ordering and for returning fact onto the nervous system in a more violent way. Why, after the great artists, do people ever try to do anything again? Only because, from generation to generation, through what the great artists have done, the instincts change. And, as the instincts change, so there comes a renewal of the feeling of how can I remake this thing once again more clearly, more exactly, more violently. You see, I believe that art is recording; I think it's reporting. And I think that in abstract art, as there's no report, there's nothing other than the aesthetic of the painter and his few sensations. There's never any tension in it.

DS  You don't think it can convey feelings?

FB  I think it can convey very watered-down lyrical feelings, because I think any shapes can. But I don't think it can really convey feeling in the grand sense.

DS  By which you mean more specific and more directed feelings?

FB  Yes.

DS  You say it lacks tension, but don't you think that certain kinds of expectation which the spectator has of art can be disturbed by an abstract painting in a way that can engender tension?

FB  I think it's possible that the onlooker can enter even more into an abstract painting. But then anybody can enter more into what is called an undisciplined emotion, because, after all, who loves a disastrous love affair or illness more than the spectator? He can enter into these things and feel he is participating and doing something about it. But that of course has nothing to do with what art is about. What you're talking about now is the entry of the spectator into the performance, and I think in abstract art perhaps they can enter more, because what they are offered is something weaker which they haven't got to combat.

DS  If abstract paintings are no more than pattern-making, how do you explain the fact that there are people like myself who have the same sort of visceral response to them at times as they have to figurative works?

FB  Fashion.

DS  You really think that?

FB  I think that only time tells about painting. No artist knows in his own lifetime whether what he does will be the slightest good, because I think it takes at least seventy-five to a hundred years before the thing begins to sort itself out from the theories that have been formed about it. And I think that most people enter a painting by the theory that has been formed about it and not by what it is. Fashion

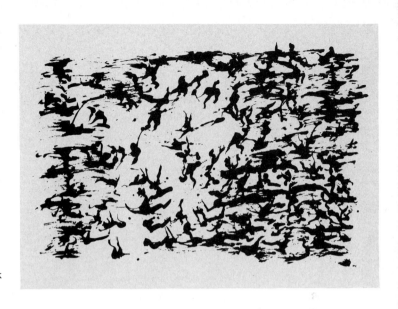

52 MICHAUX Untitled Indian ink
drawing 1962

suggests that you should be moved by certain things and
should not by others. This is the reason that even successful
artists – and especially successful artists, you may say –
have no idea whatever whether their work's any good or
not, and will never know.

DS   Not long ago you bought a picture . . .

FB   By Michaux.

DS   . . . by Michaux, which was more or less abstract. I know
you got tired of it in the end and sold it or gave it away,
but what made you buy it?

FB   Well, firstly, I don't think it's abstract. I think Michaux
is a very, very intelligent and conscious man, who is aware
of exactly the situation that he is in. And I think that he
has made the best *tachiste* or free marks that have been made.
I think he is much better in that way, in making free marks,
than Jackson Pollock.

DS   Can you say what gives you this feeling?

FB   What gives me the feeling is that it is more factual; it
suggests more. Because after all, this painting, and most of
his paintings, have always been about delayed ways of
remaking the human image, through a mark which is totally
outside an illustrational mark but yet always conveys you
back to the human image – a human image generally dragging
and trudging through deep ploughed fields, or something like

**61**

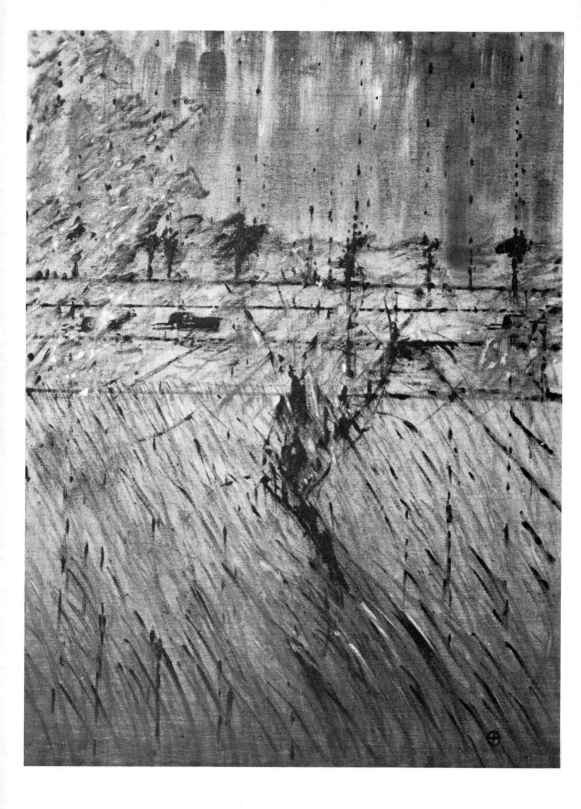

that. They are about these images moving and falling and so on.

D S   Are you ever as moved by looking at a still life or a landscape by a great master as you are by looking at paintings of the human image? Does a Cézanne still life or landscape ever move you as much as a Cézanne portrait or nude?

F B   No, it doesn't, although I think that Cézanne's landscapes are very much better than his figures, generally. I think that there are one or two figure-paintings which are marvellous, but generally speaking I think the landscapes are better.

D S   Nevertheless, the figures say more to you?

F B   They do, yes.

D S   What is it that made you paint a number of landscapes at one time?

F B   Inability to do the figure.

D S   And did you feel that you weren't going to do landscapes for long?

F B   I don't know that I felt that at the time. After all, one is always hoping that one will be able to do something nearer one's instinctive desire. But certainly landscapes interest me much less. I think art is an obsession with life and after all, as we are human beings, our greatest obsession is with ourselves. Then possibly with animals, and then with landscapes.

D S   You're really affirming the traditional hierarchy of subject matter by which history painting – painting of mythological and religious subjects – comes top and then portraits and then landscape and then still life.

F B   I would alter them round. I would say at the moment, as things are so difficult, that portraits come first.

D S   In fact, you've done very few paintings with several figures. Do you concentrate on the single figure because you find it more difficult?

F B   I think that the moment a number of figures become involved, you immediately come on to the story-telling aspect of the relationships between figures. And that immediately sets up a kind of narrative. I always hope to be able to make a great number of figures without a narrative.

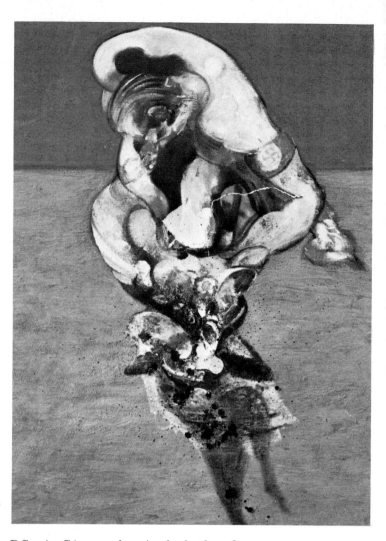

54 Detail from right-hand panel of
*41*

DS   As Cézanne does in the bathers?

FB   He does.

DS   You painted a picture not long ago which people
interpreted narratively: it was a Crucifixion triptych, and
there was a figure on the right who wore an armband with
a swastika. Now, some people thought that this was meant
to be a Nazi, and some people thought that this was not a
Nazi, but that it was like a character in Genet's play, *The
Balcony*, who had dressed up as a Nazi. Well, this was an
example of people making a narrative interpretation. I'd
like to ask, firstly, whether either of those things was meant
and, secondly, whether this was the kind of narrative
interpretation that you dislike.

FB   Well I do dislike it. It was also, you may say, a stupid thing to put the swastika there. But I wanted to put an armband to break the continuity of the arm and to add the colour of this red round the arm. You may say it was a stupid thing to do, but it was done entirely as part of trying to make the figure work – not work on the level of interpretation of its being a Nazi, but on the level of its working formally.

DS   Then why the swastika?

FB   Because I was looking at that time at some coloured photographs that I had of Hitler standing with his entourage, and all of them had these bands round their arms with a swastika.

DS   Now, when you painted this you must have known that people would see a narrative thing there, or didn't this occur to you?

FB   I think it occurred to me, but I don't think I cared much about it.

DS   And when people interpreted it narratively, did that irritate you?

FB   Not especially. Because, if I was irritated about what people said about the things, I would be in continuous irritation. I don't think it was a successful thing to do – do you see what I mean? But it was the only thing I could do at that moment.

DS   Why is it you want to avoid telling a story?

FB   I don't want to avoid telling a story, but I want very, very much to do the thing that Valéry said – to give the sensation without the boredom of its conveyance. And the moment the story enters, the boredom comes upon you.

DS   You think this necessarily happens or that you haven't been able to get outside it yet?

FB   I think I haven't been able to get outside it. I don't know who today has.

DS   Do you feel it is more difficult to paint now than it has been before?

FB   I think it is more difficult because painters had a double role before. I think that they thought that they were recording, and then they did something very much more than recording. I think that now, with the mechanical methods of recording there, such as the film and the camera and the tape recorder, you have to come down in painting to something more basic and fundamental. Because it can be done better by other means on what I think is a more superficial level – I'm not talking about film, which is cut and remade into all sorts of different things, but I'm thinking about the direct photograph and direct recording. I think that those have taken over the illustrational thing that painters in the past believed they had to do. And I think that abstract painters, realizing this, have thought: why not throw out all illustration and all forms of recording and just give the effects of form and colour? And logically this is quite right. But it hasn't worked out, because it seems that the obsession with something in life that you want to record gives a much greater tension and a much greater excitement than when you've simply said you'll just go on in a free-fancy way and record the shapes and the colours. I think we are in a very curious position today because, when there's no tradition at all, there are two extreme ends. There is direct reporting like something that's very near to a police report. And then there's only the attempt to make great art. And what is called the in-between art really, in a time like ours, doesn't exist. It doesn't mean that, in the attempt to make great art, anybody will ever do it in our time. But this is what creates an extreme situation, you may say. Because, with these marvellous mechanical means of recording fact, what can you do but go to a very much more extreme thing where you are reporting fact not as simple fact but on many levels, where you unlock the areas of feeling which lead to a deeper sense of the reality of the image, where you attempt to make the construction by which this thing will be caught raw and alive and left there and, you may say, finally fossilized – there it is.

DS   Talking about the situation in the way you do points, of course, to the very isolated position in which you're working. The isolation is obviously a great challenge, but do you also find it a frustration? Would you rather be one of a number of artists working in a similar direction?

FB   I think it would be more exciting to be one of a number of artists working together, and to be able to exchange. . . . I think it would be terribly nice to have someone to talk to. Today there is absolutely nobody to talk to. Perhaps I'm unlucky and don't know those people. Those I know always have very different attitudes to what I have. But I think that artists can in fact help one another. They can clarify the situation to one another. I've always thought of friendship as where two people really tear one another apart and perhaps in that way learn something from one another.

DS  Have you ever got anything from what's called destructive criticism made by critics?

FB  I think that destructive criticism, especially by other artists, is certainly the most helpful criticism. Even if, when you analyze it, you may feel that it's wrong, at least you analyze it and think about it. When people praise you, well, it's very pleasant to be praised, but it doesn't actually help you.

DS  Do you find you can bring yourself to make destructive criticism of your friends' work?

FB  Unfortunately, with most of them I can't if I want to keep them as friends.

DS  Do you find you can criticize their personalities and keep them as friends?

FB  It's easier, because people are less vain of their personalities than they are of their work. They feel in an odd way, I think, that they're not irrevocably committed to their personality, that they can work on it and change it, whereas the work that has gone out – nothing can be done about it. But I've always hoped to find another painter I could really talk to – somebody whose qualities and sensibility I'd really believe in – who really tore my things to bits and whose judgement I could actually believe in. I envy very much, for instance, going to another art, I envy very much the situation when Eliot and Pound and Yeats were all working together. And in fact Pound made a kind of caesarean operation on *The Waste Land*; he also had a very strong influence on Yeats – although both of them may have been very much better poets than Pound. I think it would be marvellous to have somebody who would say to you, 'Do this, do that, don't do this, don't do that!' and give you the reasons. I think it would be very helpful.

DS  You feel you really could use that kind of help?

FB  I could. Very much. Yes. I long for people to tell me what to do, to tell me where I go wrong. □ □ □

# 3

DS   You didn't start painting full-time till quite late.

FB   I couldn't. When I was young, I didn't, in a sense, have a real subject. It's through my life and knowing other people that a subject has really grown. Also, perhaps it delayed me, never going to any art school or anything like that, although in many ways I think that could have been an advantage – I don't think art schools can do anything for artists today. But there are certain things I regret very much – for instance, not learning ancient Greek – but of course it's very much later that I regret it.

DS   When do you think painting became central in your life?

FB   I think it became central, really, from around 1945. As you know, through asthma and everything else, I was turned down from going into the army. And I think in those years Eric Hall had a great influence on me and encouraged me. But then he had a great influence altogether on my life, as he was an intelligent man and had a lot of sensibility. I mean, he taught me the value of things – for instance, what decent food was – that I certainly didn't learn in Ireland; the thing I appreciate from Ireland is the kind of freedom of life.

DS   When you started designing furniture and rugs in the late 1920s, you were immediately doing work that was exceptional; and it was thought to be so at the time.

FB   Yes, but it was just taken from other people, most of it. It was awfully influenced by French design of that time. I don't think anything was very original.

55 (Opposite) Furniture and rugs designed by Bacon, photographed in his studio 1930

DS   And you had no interest in going on and trying to do something more original?

68

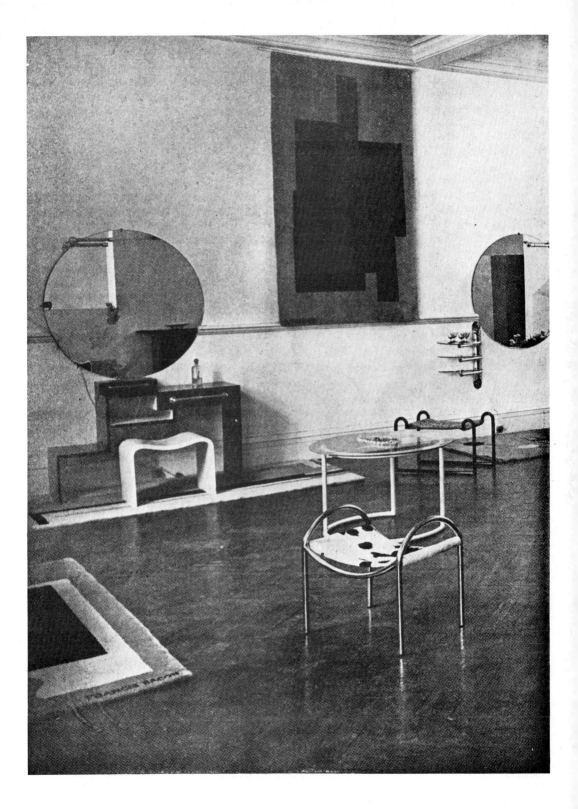

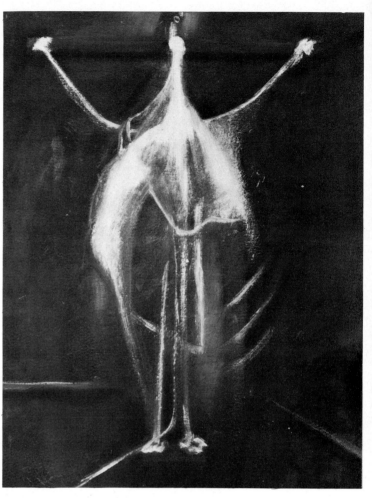

56 *Crucifixion* 1933

FB   No. I started to try and do painting.

DS   But there again, it didn't take long before you were doing exceptional work, like the *Crucifixion* which Herbert Read reproduced in *Art Now* in 1933. Nevertheless, you didn't paint a great deal in the following years, did you?

FB   No, I didn't. I enjoyed myself.

DS   But did you realize painting was going to become . . .?

FB   Not till much later, no. I regret now that I was such a late starter – I seem to have been a late starter in everything. I think I was kind of delayed, and I think there are those people who are delayed.

DS   You talk of delay though you did remarkable work as a designer and as a painter in your early twenties.

70

FB   I think the analytic side of my brain didn't develop till comparatively late – till I was about twenty-seven or twenty-eight. When I was very young, you see, I was incredibly shy, and later I thought it was ridiculous to be shy, so I tried deliberately to get over this because I think old shy people are ridiculous. And when I was thirty or so I gradually began to be able to open myself out. But most people do it at a much younger age. So I always feel I wasted so many years of my life.

DS   When you say you didn't have a subject, are you saying it from hindsight or were you aware of it at the time?

FB   No, I say it through hindsight. But I always thought of those paintings from Velasquez as a failure, and that was perhaps one of the first subjects that I had. I became obsessed by this painting and I bought photograph after photograph of it. I think really that was my first subject.

DS   And that began in the late 1940s. Do you think your involvement in it had something to do with feelings about your father?

FB   I'm not quite sure I understand what you're saying.

DS   Well, the Pope is *il Papa.*

FB   Well, I certainly have never thought of it in that way, but I don't know – it's difficult to know what forms obsessions. The thing is, I never got on with either my mother or my father. They didn't want me to be a painter, they thought I was just a drifter, especially my mother. It was only when she began to realize that I was making some money out of it – and that was very late in her life and not so long before she died – that we made any contact and she altered her attitude; also my father had died and she had remarried twice and had changed a great deal. My father was very narrow-minded. He was an intelligent man who never developed his intellect at all. As you know, he was a trainer of racehorses. And he just fought with people. He really had no friends at all, because he fought with everybody, because he had this very opinionated attitude. And he certainly didn't get on with his children. I think he liked my youngest brother, who died when he was about fourteen. He certainly didn't get on with me.

DS   And what were your feelings towards him?

FB   Well, I disliked him, but I was sexually attracted to him

71

when I was young. When I first sensed it, I hardly knew it was sexual. It was only later, through the grooms and the people in the stables I had affairs with, that I realized that it was a sexual thing towards my father.

DS So perhaps the obsession with the Velasquez Pope had a strong personal meaning?

FB Well it's one of the most beautiful pictures in the world and I think I'm not at all exceptional as a painter in being obsessed by it. I think a number of artists have recognized it as being something very remarkable.

DS I don't think other painters have continued to make versions of it over and over again.

FB I wish I hadn't.

DS Of course, you often combined the Pope theme with another theme that you'd started using earlier – actually, I'd have expected you to say that either this or the Crucifixion was your first subject – the open mouth, the scream.

FB When I made the Pope screaming, I didn't do it in the way I wanted to. I was always, as I've said to you before, very obsessed by Monet, and I think I was obsessed by Monet even at a time when people weren't, because I remember that, when I said things about him, people said 'Oh, they're just a lot of ice-creams', and they couldn't see. Before that, I'd bought that very beautiful hand-coloured book on diseases of the mouth, and, when I made the Pope screaming, I didn't want to do it in the way that I did it – I wanted to make the mouth, with the beauty of its colour and everything, look like one of the sunsets or something of Monet, and not just the screaming Pope. If I did it again, which I hope to God I never will, I would make it like a Monet.

DS And not the black cavern which in fact. . . .

FB Yes, not the black cavern.

DS I suppose the most crucial step in the development of your subject-matter came in the early 1950s when you started to do paintings of particular people you knew, whereas previously you'd mainly been doing variations on existing images. And you did them sometimes working from memory and sometimes from snapshots and quite often at first from the model. Was it a technical problem or a psychological one that had prevented you from doing that earlier?

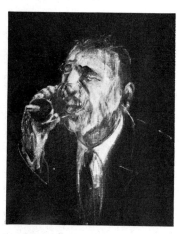

57 *Man Drinking (Portrait of David Sylvester)* 1955

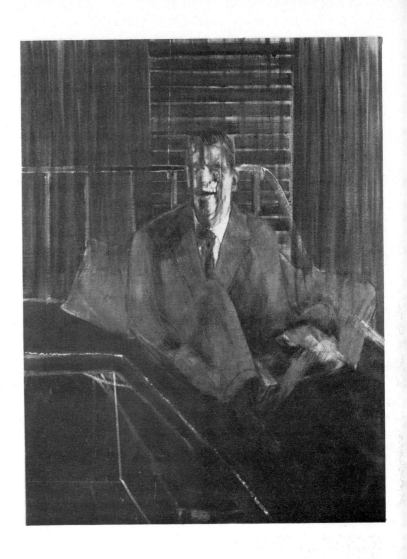

58 *Study for a Portrait* 1953

FB   I think a technical problem.

DS   It was easier to work from existing images than from a person or the memory of a person?

FB   Yes.

DS   Of course, in painting particular persons you've worked a lot from photographs of them.

FB   Yes, but they're always people I've known very well, and the photographs are only used to make me remember their features, to revise my memory of them, as one would use a dictionary, really. I couldn't do people I didn't know very well. I wouldn't want to. It wouldn't interest me to try

**73**

and do them unless I had seen a lot of them, watched their contours, watched the way they behaved.

DS  In the same period as you were starting to paint particular people, you also did your first two paintings of figures coupled – the ones on a bed in 1953 and the ones in a field in 1954. And then it was about twelve years before you did more paintings of this theme, but since you started again it's been almost your dominant subject.

FB  Well, of course, it's an endless subject, isn't it? You need never have any other subject, really. It's a very haunting subject, and I should be able to do it in a quite different way now – in the way I was going to do it when I had the idea of doing sculptures. Whether I will ever do them or

59 *Two Figures* 1953

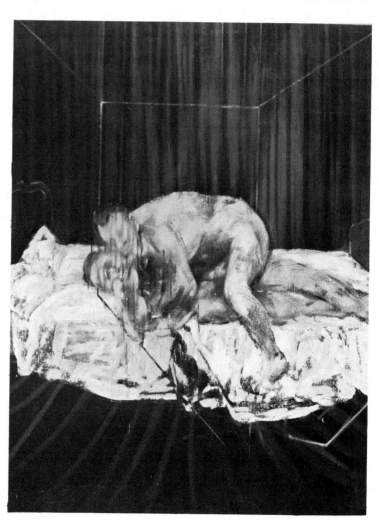

60 (Opposite) *Two Figures in the Grass* 1954

74

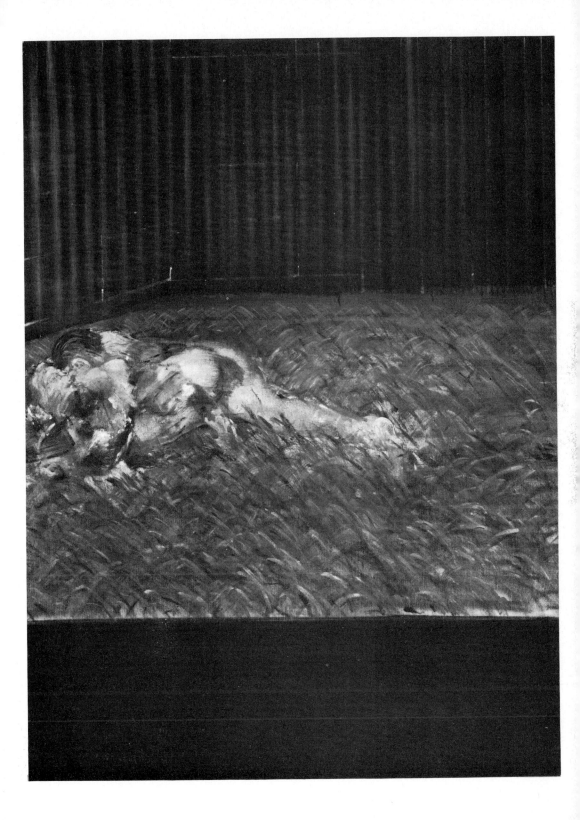

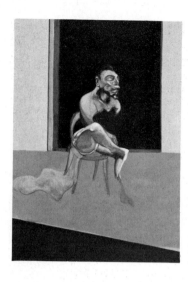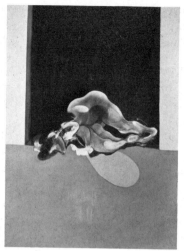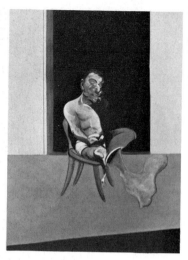

61 *Triptych – August 1972*

not is a different story, but I think I would be able to do the figures in a really different way by painting them as a transposition of how I was going to do them in the sculptures. I wasn't only going to do those kinds of figures in the sculptures, but also all sorts of things of the human body, and I can see that I can start in another way altogether now, now that I feel exorcized – although one's never exorcized, because people say you forget about death, but you don't. After all, I've had a very unfortunate life, because all the people I've been really fond of have died. And you don't stop thinking about them; time doesn't heal. But you concentrate on something which was an obsession, and what you would have put into your obsession with the physical act you put into your work. Because one of the terrible things about so-called love, certainly for an artist, I think, is the destruction. But I think without it they could probably never have. . . . I absolutely don't know. I was talking to somebody the other day and I said: 'Supposing one had just lived in a cottage somewhere and had had no experiences at all, all one's life, would one perhaps do exactly the same thing or better?' I think not, but I sometimes do wonder. □ □ □

DS   One thing that's always struck me about you is that, when you're talking about people you know, you tend to analyze how they've behaved or would be likely to behave in an extreme situation, and to judge them in that light. Are you aware you do that?

62 (Opposite) Centre panel of *61*

76

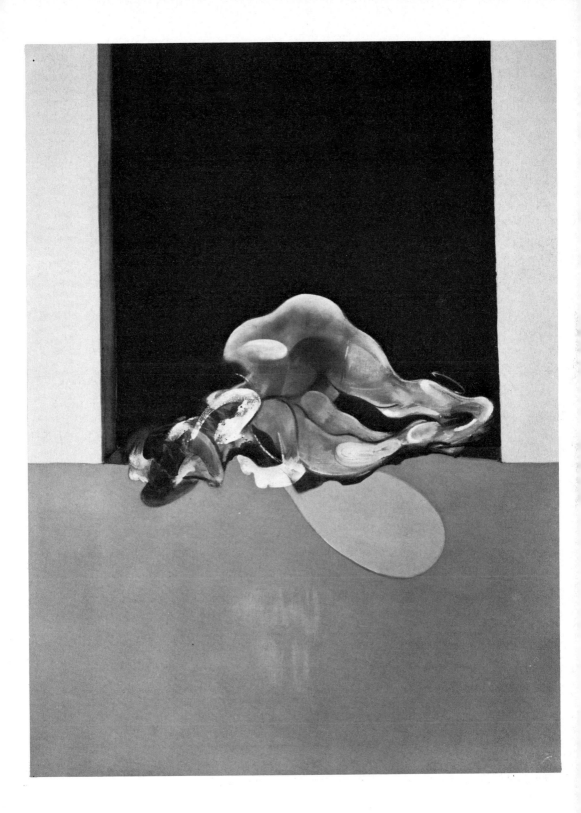

FB   I suppose I'm aware, though I wasn't aware in the very distinct way in which you put it. But I think it's an indication of people's, you may say, qualities how they behave in an extreme situation.

DS   Well, it seems to me that that preoccupation of yours is very relevant to your work, either overtly or implicitly. Overtly when you paint the scream – and you even impose the scream on that cool Velasquez Pope – and the Crucifixion, and people violently coupling on beds, and single figures in convulsive attitudes, and nudes injecting drugs into their arms.

FB   I've used the figures lying on beds with a hypodermic syringe as a form of nailing the image more strongly into reality or appearance. I don't put the syringe because of the drug that's being injected but because it's less stupid than putting a nail through the arm, which would be even more melodramatic. I put the syringe because I want a nailing of the flesh onto the bed. But that, perhaps, is something I shall pass out of entirely.

DS   Now, I wouldn't want to make too much of your overtly dramatic subjects, because, after all, a great deal of European art represents moments of high drama. What I feel is conclusive is that, when you paint a man simply sitting in a room or walking down the street, almost everyone who looks at the paintings seems to feel that this is anything but a banal or neutral situation, but that this figure is involved in some kind of crisis, perhaps some apprehension of impending doom.

FB   I think you once said to me that people always have a feeling of mortality about my paintings.

DS   Yes.

FB   But then, perhaps, I have a feeling of mortality all the time. Because, if life excites you, its opposite, like a shadow, death, must excite you. Perhaps not excite you, but you are aware of it in the same way as you are aware of life, you're aware of it like the turn of a coin between life and death. And I'm very aware of that about people, and about myself too, after all. I'm always surprised when I wake up in the morning.

63 (Opposite) *Lying Figure with Hypodermic Syringe* 1963

DS   Doesn't that belie your view that you're essentially an optimistic person?

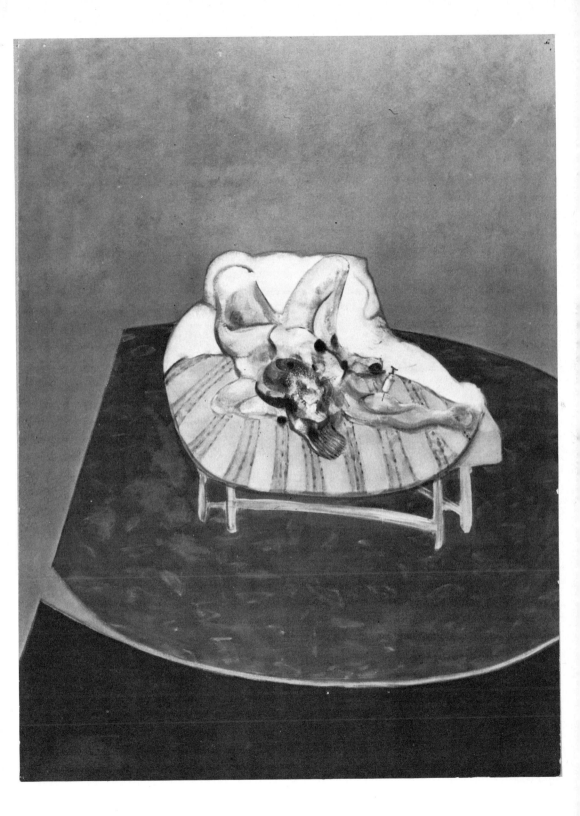

FB  Ah well, you can be optimistic and totally without hope. One's basic nature is totally without hope, and yet one's nervous system is made out of optimistic stuff. It doesn't make any difference to my awareness of the shortness of the moment of existence between birth and death. And that's one thing I'm conscious of all the time. And I suppose it does come through in my paintings.

DS  It does come through.

FB  But does it more than in other people's paintings today?

DS  Well, of course, there's not all that number who are painting the figure today. But I think it does more. And people seem to feel in looking at your figures that they are seen in moments of crisis, moments of acute awareness of their mortality, moments of acute awareness of their animal nature – moments of recognition of what might be called elemental truths about themselves.

FB  But surely any art is always made up of those qualities?

DS  Well, it's possibly true, say, of Rembrandt.

FB  I find it true of every art that I know of that has interested me. But then I hope we're not talking at cross purposes, because we know it so well we read it into everything else too.

DS  Well, it's not a quality which we get in looking at a Renoir. You might say that you're not particularly interested in Renoir.

FB  Oh, I think Renoir did most beautiful landscapes. I'm not certain that I'm so interested in the figures. But, on the other hand, if one has that attitude to life that I have, and I think you probably have too, one can feel it even in these figures which appear bathed in this wonderful light of happiness on a summer afternoon. So in a sense I would be aware of it, I think, in Renoir as I would be in Degas or in Rembrandt or in Velasquez. One is particularly aware of it in Velasquez, of course. I don't know whether it's because of Velasquez's tremendous sophistication. Obviously, he was a profoundly sophisticated man living in the society of the Court, and he was probably the only really sophisticated being existing around the Court at the time; that was the reason the King insisted on keeping him near him, because he was the only man that at least enlivened for a moment his

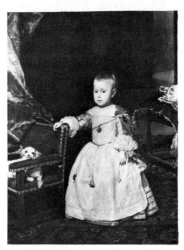

64 VELASQUEZ *Prince Philip Prosper* 1659

day. But one feels in all his paintings the whole poignancy that Velasquez must have felt – even in those beautiful things where the figures have this wonderful structure and yet at the same time have the colouring of a Monet. You feel the shadow of life passing all the time.

DS   But the intimations of mortality in Velasquez or Degas or even Rembrandt aren't conveyed with anything of the menace with which they are in your work, where most people seem to feel there's somehow a distinct presence or threat of violence.

FB   Well, there might be one reason for this, of course. I was born in Ireland, in 1909. My father, because he was a racehorse trainer, lived not very far from the Curragh, where there was a British cavalry regiment, and I always remember them, just before the 1914 war was starting, galloping up the drive of the house which my father had and carrying out manoeuvres. And then I was brought to London during the war and spent quite a lot of time there, because my father was in the War Office then, and I was made aware of what is called the possibility of danger even at a very young age. Then I went back to Ireland and was brought up during the Sinn Fein movement. And I lived for a time with my grandmother, who married the Commissioner of Police for Kildare amongst her numerous marriages, and we lived in a sandbagged house and, as I went out, these ditches were dug across the road for a car or horse-and-cart or anything like that to fall into, and there would be snipers waiting on the edges. And then, when I was sixteen or seventeen, I went to Berlin, and of course I saw the Berlin of 1927 and 1928 where there was a wide open city, which was, in a way, very, very violent. Perhaps it was violent to me because I had come from Ireland, which was violent in the military sense but not violent in the emotional sense, in the way Berlin was. And after Berlin I went to Paris, and then I lived all those disturbed years between then and the war which started in 1939. So I could say, perhaps, I have been accustomed to always living through forms of violence – which may or may not have an effect upon one, but I think probably does. But this violence of my life, the violence which I've lived amongst, I think it's different to the violence in painting. When talking about the violence of paint, it's nothing to do with the violence of war. It's to do with an attempt to remake the violence of reality itself. And the violence of reality is not only the simple violence meant when you say that a rose or something is violent, but it's the violence also of the suggestions within the image itself which can only be conveyed through paint. When I look at you across the table, I don't only see you but I see a whole emanation which has to do with personality and everything else. And to put that over in a painting, as I would like to be able to do in a portrait, means that it would appear violent in paint. We nearly always live through screens – a screened existence. And I sometimes think, when people say my work looks violent, that perhaps I have from time to time been able to clear away one or two of the veils or screens.

DS   One thing that's clear is that you're not concerned in your painting to say something about the nature of man, in the way that an artist like, say, Munch was.

FB   I'm certainly not. I'm just trying to make images as accurately off my nervous system as I can. I don't even know what half of them mean. I'm not saying anything. Whether one's saying anything for other people, I don't know. But I'm not really saying anything, because I'm probably much more concerned with the aesthetic qualities of a work than, perhaps, Munch was. But I've no idea what any artist is trying to say, except the most banal artists; I can think what Fuseli and people like that are trying to say.

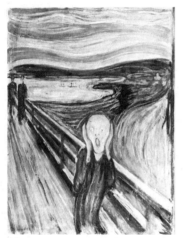

65 MUNCH *The Scream* 1893

DS   Perhaps the tendency to interpret your work as saying something comes from the fact that people like to try and find a story in art and are rather starved of stories in the art of our time, so that, when they find an art like yours, it's a great temptation to weave stories.

FB   Yes, I'm sure it is.

DS   Something similar has happened with Giacometti – the tendency to interpret his figures as Existential Man.

FB   And how did he feel about that?

DS   He thought it was rather crass. He said he was only trying to copy what he saw.

FB   Exactly.

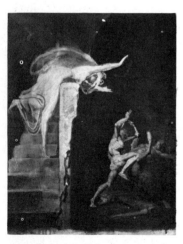

66 FUSELI *Ariadne Watching the Struggle of Theseus with the Minotaur* c. 1815

DS   On the other hand, he wasn't only copying what he saw. He was, for one thing, crystallizing very complex feelings about the act of seeing, especially about gazing at someone

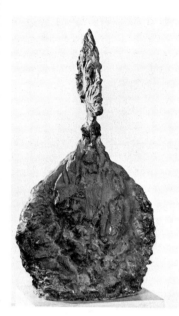

67 GIACOMETTI *Head of Diego* 1955

who is gazing back at you. Perhaps you'd tell me what you feel your painting is concerned with besides appearance.

FB   It's concerned with my kind of psyche, it's concerned with my kind of – I'm putting it in a very pleasant way – exhilarated despair. □ □ □

DS   Those sculptures you used to talk about wanting to do: have you more or less given up the idea now?

FB   I don't think I will do them, because I think I have now found a way by which I could do the images I thought of more satisfactorily in paint than I could in sculpture. I haven't started on them yet, but through thinking about them as sculptures it suddenly came to me how I could make them in paint, and do them much better in paint. It would be a kind of structured painting in which images, as it were, would arise from a river of flesh. It sounds a terribly romantic idea, but I see it very formally.

DS   And what would the form be?

FB   They would certainly be raised on structures.

DS   Several figures?

FB   Yes, and there would probably be a pavement raised high out of its naturalistic setting, out of which they could move as though out of pools of flesh rose the images, if possible, of specific people walking on their daily round. I hope to be able to do figures arising out of their own flesh with their bowler hats and their umbrellas and make them figures as poignant as a Crucifixion.

DS   And you'd do it on single canvases or in triptychs?

FB   I'd do it on a canvas; I might do triptychs of it.

DS   Up to now, you've always worked – leaving aside about two exceptions – with the canvas upright, never horizontal, so that, when you've done a horizontal work, it's invariably been a triptych. Have you ever had visions of paintings you might do on a single horizontal canvas of about the same size as the large triptychs?

FB   Yes, I have. I was only thinking today about that very thing – that I just might alter the whole dimensions of the canvases. I might easily do that. But I shall have to move into another studio to do it, because nothing larger will go through my place – not even half an inch larger. Though that isn't the reason I've done triptychs.

DS  When you're working on them, you don't have the three canvases up together; you do them separately?

FB  I do them separately. But I know how I want them to be from the point of view of scale, one against the other, and therefore it's only a question of taking small measurements.

DS  And you work on them separately to the point of completing one before going on to the next?

FB  Generally.

DS  After finishing the third one, do you ever go back and make modifications to the first two?

FB  Yes.

DS  Triptychs have been a very large part of your output in recent years. Of course, your very first major work was a triptych, back in 1944 (3). But, oddly enough, between then and 1962, I think you only did one, of heads, in 1953 – and I remember that you painted the right-hand canvas as a self-sufficient work and that I tried to sell it for you to two or three different dealers for about £60 and failed (though it was one of the best things you'd ever done) and that you then painted the other two canvases. But over the last ten years you've been doing triptychs more and more. What attracts you so much to the form?

FB  I see images in series. And I suppose I could go on long beyond the triptych and do five or six together, but I find the triptych is a more balanced unit.

DS  But, given a room with wallspace for six separate large canvases, if you were asked to do a series of six paintings to hang there permanently, would you find that an attractive idea?

FB  Yes, very.

DS  But, when the series is to be a unit, you find the triptych enough. Now, I can see what you mean about the balance in relation to the large triptychs, because in these you quite often make the two outside canvases rather similar to each other in design – sometimes almost mirror-images of each other – and use a contrasting kind of composition in the central canvas. But in the triptychs of heads you just have

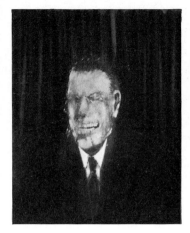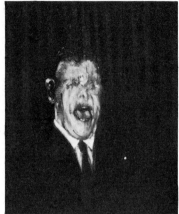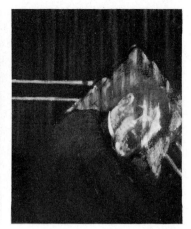

68 *Three Studies of the Human Head* 1953

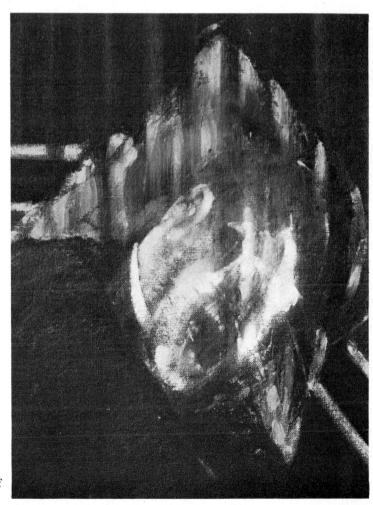

69 Detail from right-hand panel of *68*

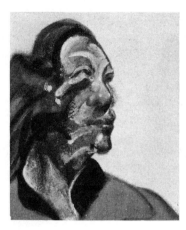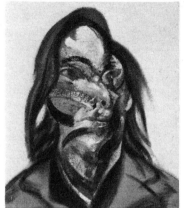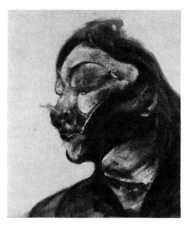

70 *Three Studies of Isabel Rawsthorne on Light Ground* 1965

a row of heads, and one can easily imagine the row's being extended – especially as you've sometimes done a series of four heads on separate canvases and you also once put four, like a strip of film, on a single canvas. So it's interesting that you've never done a polyptych of four or five heads.

FB Well, I've sometimes thought of it. On the other hand, in the triptychs I get them rather like police records, looking side face, front face, and then side face from the other side.

DS I take it that in the triptychs it's important for you that each canvas should be contained within a frame?

FB Well, there was something very unsatisfactory, for instance, when I had the show in Paris and the Guggenheim lent their *Crucifixion* triptych (*8*) and the canvases were all together in one frame. It absolutely ruined the whole picture. I wrote and told them that if I'd wanted them all to be together I would have put them together. I wanted them to be in separate frames. It ruins the balance putting them together, because, if I'd wanted to do that, I would have painted them a different way. Whether they've been changed back . . . I don't suppose so. They always think that they know best.

DS Speaking of the way the work is shown, how about the glass? I know you always like to have the paintings under glass, but, when there are those large dark areas, and one sees oneself reflected in them – and also furniture and also pictures on the opposite wall – it does become very difficult to see what's there. Are the reflections something you positively want to have, or are they something to be put up with?

FB  I don't want them to be there; I feel that they should be put up with. I feel that, because I use no varnishes or anything of that kind, and because of the very flat way I paint, the glass helps to unify the picture. I also like the distance between what has been done and the onlooker that the glass creates; I like, as it were, the removal of the object as far as possible.

DS  So it's not that you feel that the reflections add something by adding to the scrambling of the forms?

FB  Well, oddly enough, I even like Rembrandts under glass. And it's true to say in many ways they're more difficult to see, but you can still look into them.

DS  Do you feel, perhaps, that having to look through the reflections forces one to look harder? Is that a factor?

FB  No, it isn't. It's the distance – that this thing is shut away from the spectator.

DS  When looking at Duchamp's *Large Glass*, one can also look through it and see other people and other paintings in the room at the same time as the forms on the glass. Now, in a way, through the reflections, something of the same confusion is got by your use of glass. But I take it that there's no attempt to get that.

FB  There is no attempt to do what Duchamp did, which was a perfectly logical thing. Whereas to want the person reflected in the glass of a dark painting is illogical and has no meaning. I think it's just one of those misfortunes. I hope they'll make glass soon which doesn't reflect.

DS  Of course, the non-reflecting glass that's been produced so far has that unfortunate effect of acting like frosted glass.

FB  There's very little reflection in perspex, but it actually sucks the paint off the canvas. You can rub it with anti-magnetic things, but that doesn't really work.

DS  I'm told that a lot of private collectors of your work remove the glass.

FB  Yes. It's the fashion to see paintings without glass nowadays. If they want to remove it, that's their business, of course. I can't stop them.

DS  Do you have any feelings as to whether you prefer works of yours to be in private houses or in museums?

FB  I really don't mind. What I do like is space, and it depends on the space of the private house, really, or the space of the museum. I think that my paintings work better with a lot of space around them.

DS  But you don't mind at all whether they're in private or in public hands and which particular hands?

FB  I don't. They've gone out, and I know the ones that I like and the ones that I don't like and it doesn't worry me that my things should be seen or should be what is called appreciated. It doesn't mean anything to me. I'm glad if somebody likes them, of course, but I can't say it's a worrying thing for me at all. I believe people do actually worry who buys their paintings and where they're going to be put, but it doesn't really worry me. Perhaps I'm not public-spirited. I don't care. I would be annoyed if, for instance, people bought the things that I liked best and just destroyed them – burnt them or something like that.

DS  Why would you be annoyed?

FB  I would be annoyed because, for myself, I would like, if anything remains of mine when I'm dead, I would like the best images to remain.

DS  But why?

FB  That's just vanity. It's a thing that one will never know about because one will be dead, but nevertheless, if my things do last at all, I would like the best things to last.

DS  Well, then, you mind a bit that your things should be seen.

FB  When I say I care, I care because – I can only talk from an absolutely personal view – I think some of the images I have made have for me got a kind of potency about them, and so, you may say, I care that those ones should remain. But, if I think really logically, it's stupid to think even that way, because I simply won't know anything about it, any more than these people who fuss in their lifetime about whether their things are good, really, or bad, because they won't ever know. Because time is the only great critic.

DS  Even so, in Shakespeare's sonnets, for example, again and again the final couplet makes the point that, long after he is dead, these lines will still be read.

FB  Yes, true.

DS   There's a paradox about the survival of works of art —
I mean in our society, where art doesn't serve any ritual or
didactic purpose. The motivation to do it is the doing of it,
the excitement of solving problems, but problems of a kind
that can only be solved through actually making something,
so that, at the end of the process, there's this thing, the
residue of the activity. Now, once having made that thing,
the artist really might as well destroy it, but usually he seems
to prefer to let it go on existing.

FB   Well, there are two reasons for not destroying. One is
that, unless you are a rich man, you want if you can to live by
something it really absorbs you to try and do. The other is
that one doesn't know how far the will to make this thing
hasn't got already leaked into it the stupidity, you may say,
of the idea of immortality. After all, to be an artist at all is
a form of vanity. And that vanity may be washed over by this
rationally futile idea of immortality. It would also be a vanity
to suggest that what one does oneself might help to thicken
life. But, of course, we do know that our lives have been
thickened by great art. One of the very few ways in which
life has been really thickened is by the great things that a
few people have left. Well, art is, of course, a profoundly
vain occupation, really.

DS   Nowadays you allow a far higher proportion of your
work to survive than you did twenty years ago.

FB   I only think or hope that I've got a bit better.

DS   You don't need to do so for financial reasons, I imagine,
because the prices are so much higher now that you could
probably live by releasing one or two works a year.

FB   Yes, I could.

DS   So you obviously feel that the work is more worth
preserving?

FB   I just hope that I'm going to do something so much
better.

DS   In the past, it was very often the best works that were
destroyed, because, since they were good, you wanted to
take them further, and then the paint would get clogged and
you couldn't extricate them. Does this happen less than it
used to do?

FB   Well, I've become much more technically wily about

those sorts of bogs that I used to fall into, as you say, with the better things by trying to take them further. I can manipulate the paint now in a way that I don't have to get into the kind of marshland which I can't extricate myself from. I do go on working on them, but I do, of course, work very much more by chance now than I did when I was young. For instance, I throw an awful lot of paint onto things, and I don't know what is going to happen to it. But I do it much more than I used to.

DS   Do you throw it with a brush?

FB   No, I throw it with my hand. I just squeeze it into my hand and throw it on.

DS   I remember you used to use a rag a lot.

FB   I do use it a lot too, still. I use anything. I use scrubbing brushes and sweeping brushes and any of those things that I think painters have used. They've always used everything. I don't know, but I'm certain Rembrandt used an enormous amount of things.

DS   When you throw paint, the image has reached a certain state and you want to push it further?

FB   Yes, and I can't by my will push it further. I can only hope that the throwing of the paint onto the already-made image or half-made image will either re-form the image or that I will be able to manipulate this paint further into – anyway, for me – a greater intensity.

DS   I know this is an impossible question because it can't be answered in a general way, but, very broadly speaking, do you tend to throw paint quite often in the course of working on a picture, or once in a couple of hours, or what?

FB   Well, that is difficult. It might happen quite often, or it might happen only once and the thing comes more right, if you see what I mean, and I don't need to throw it again.

DS   And what about the use of scrubbing brushes and rags and so on? Do you tend to use a rag fairly continually?

FB   Yes.

DS   To rub out what you've put?

FB   No, not to rub out. I impregnate rags with colour, and they leave this kind of network of colour across the image. I use them nearly always.

DS   Can you conceive of getting to a stage where you had such freedom in your handling of the brush that it became unnecessary to interrupt the process with other practices?

FB   But I use those other practices just to disrupt it. I'm always trying to disrupt it. Half my painting activity is disrupting what I can do with ease.

DS   About this problem of chance, an example of a work made very much according to chance would be Duchamp's *Three Standard Stoppages* of 1913, where he took three threads each a metre in length, dropped each of them from the height of a metre onto a separate canvas stained Prussian blue, and fixed them there as they had fallen. Now, however much the concept of this work reflects a very idiosyncratic

71 Duchamp *Three Standard Stoppages* 1913–14

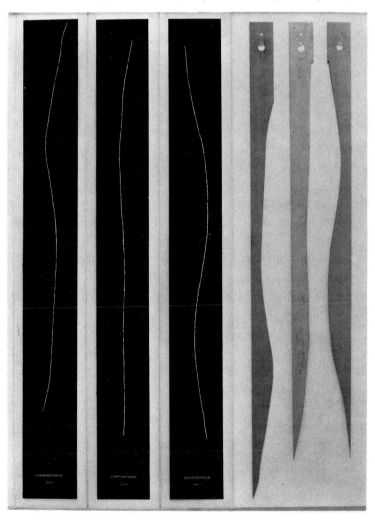

genius, when it came to the random factor it seems likely that Duchamp could have asked his cleaner to come in and drop the threads. But could you ask your cleaner to come in, take a handful of paint, and at a certain moment, chosen by you, throw it at the canvas? Is it conceivable that she might get useful results?

FB Quite conceivable. But she would probably think it was immoral and she wouldn't do it.

DS In other words, you're saying that the throwing of the paint really is random?

FB Yes.

DS But if someone other than yourself were given the moment when to throw the paint and the choice of what paint to throw, what colour to throw, what consistency to throw, there'd be an enormous amount of decision on your part, even allowing that somebody else could throw the paint as usefully as you could.

FB I know the part of the canvas I want to throw at, so I would have to tell them what part of the canvas to throw at, and, since I've thrown an awful lot, perhaps I'd know how to aim better onto that part. But I'm not suggesting that somebody else couldn't come in and throw it and might not then create another image altogether or a better image. I'm always hoping for that. But I don't think, perhaps, my paintings look like that. For instance, I would loathe my paintings to look like chancy abstract expressionist paintings, because I really like highly disciplined painting, although I don't use highly disciplined methods of constructing it. I think the only thing is that my paint looks immediate. Perhaps it's a vanity to say that, but at least I sometimes think, in the better things, the paint has an immediacy, although I don't think it looks like thrown-about paint.

DS But this chance is really very controlled when you come to think of it. Because, apart from the moment of decision as to when to throw, and apart from the consistency and choice of colour, and apart from the choice of the part of the painting at which it is to be thrown, there is also the angle and force at which it is to be thrown, which obviously depends very much on practice and knowing the kinds of things that happen when the paint is thrown at a certain velocity and at a certain angle.

92

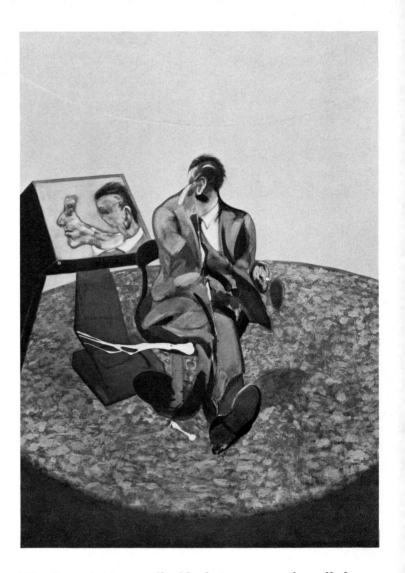

72 *Portrait of George Dyer in a Mirror* 1968

FB   But paint is so malleable that you never do really know. It's such an extraordinary supple medium that you never do quite know what paint will do. I mean, you even don't know that when you put it on wilfully, as it were, with a brush – you never quite know how it will go on. I think you probably know more with acrylic paint, which all the new painters use.

DS   You don't use acrylic at all?

FB   I do use acrylic sometimes for the background.

DS   But do you not feel that with experience you are more aware of the kinds of thing that are likely to happen when you throw paint?

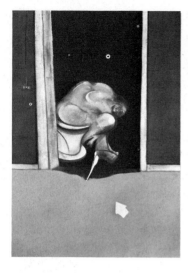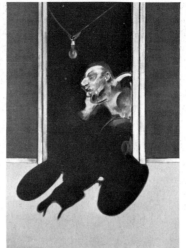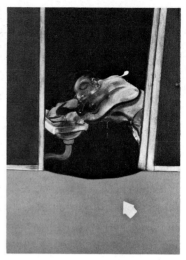

73 *Triptych – May-June 1973*

**FB** Not necessarily. Because I very often throw it and then take a great sponge or rag and sponge it out, and that in itself leaves another totally different kind of form. You see, I want the paintings to come about so that they look as though the marks had a sort of inevitability about them. I hate that kind of sloppy sort of Central European painting. It's one of the reasons I don't really like abstract expressionism. Quite apart from its being abstract, I just don't like the sloppiness of it.

**DS** It's like what you said before; it's using chance to get a controlled-looking result. And, in fact, it is always highly controlled, inasmuch as you would never end a painting by suddenly throwing something at it. Or would you?

**FB** Oh yes. In that recent triptych, on the shoulder of the figure being sick into the basin, there's like a whip of white paint that goes like that. Well, I did that at the very last moment, and I just left it. I don't know if it's right, but for me it looked right.

**DS** Now, had it not looked right, could you have taken the knife and removed it?

**FB** I could. As that background is a very thinly painted mixture of Prussian blue and black, I could have taken the knife. I would then have had to scrub it, that background, and reapply the paint, because I wanted it to be very thin and I'd have had to just try again and see. This just happened – well, at least, I thought – right. Of course Frank Auerbach

74 (Opposite) Right-hand panel of 73

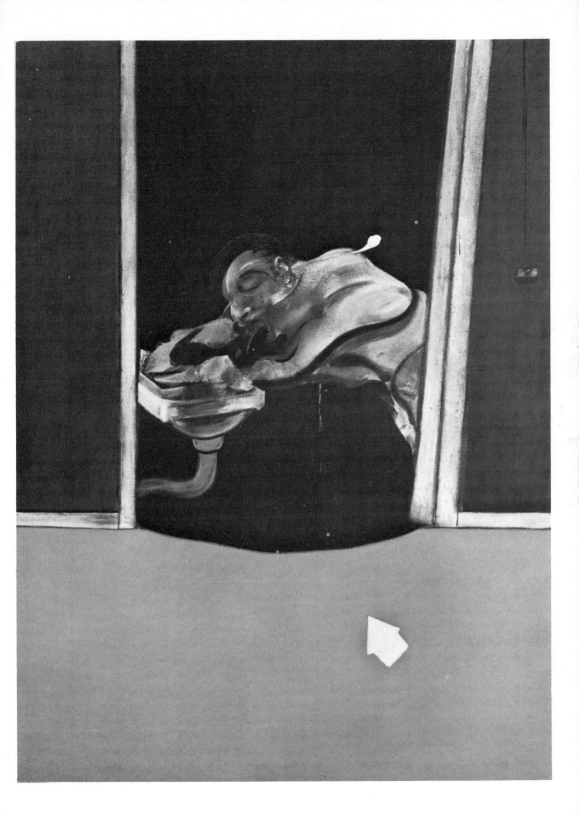

says what I call accident isn't accident at all. But then what else can I call it?

DS   What does he say it is?

FB   Well, you see, he can't define what it is, if it's not accident and chance. He can't define what it is. Can you?

DS   Well, there is something that I wonder whether it's like, and that is this strange feeling you sometimes get in playing ball games, when you play a shot and feel that you didn't play the shot but it played you. Now, obviously you can only play a shot like that when you've practiced your swing and have got your action into a certain groove. And then suddenly in the middle of a game somebody will play a very good shot and in reply you will play a better shot than you thought you could ever possibly play. The very difficulty makes your own shot that much better, and you're amazed and don't know how you did it, hardly believe you did it.

FB   Exactly.

DS   And obviously there was no way of preparing for it, there wasn't time, and the very fact that there wasn't time made the shot play itself.

FB   Well, it is in a way inspired chance when those things happen. Of course it's based on the fact that you know a great deal about the game you're playing. But nevertheless you wouldn't probably have done that particular thing by will-power.

DS   Absolutely not. You'd have tensed up. But of course in making art, and this also applies to playing games, there is a kind of trance-like state you can get into. I imagine that Cézanne was talking about that kind of state when he said that, if he took thought when painting, everything was lost. Do you feel you're in that kind of state when things are going well?

FB   I don't like using the word trance-like nowadays, because it comes too near to modern mysticism, which I hate. I also think, perhaps, it sounds slightly pompous to say it's a trance-like state; do you know what I mean?

DS   Yes, indeed, I know it's slightly pompous, but I don't know what else one could say.

FB   No, it's very difficult.

DS   It's acting by instinct.

FB  It is. But then all art surely is instinct, and then you can't talk about instinct, because you don't know what it is.

DS  But it's an instinct rooted in cultivation and practice and knowledge.

FB  I think so. Because we know, for instance, the instinctive art of children, but yet it's a totally different type of instinct, and very unsatisfactory finally.

DS  Now, as to the interaction between, say, throwing paint at the canvas and then manipulating that paint, I raised the question before whether the cleaner could come and do the throwing equally well if she had no inhibitions about doing it and followed your instructions. But I'm now going to say that maybe the cleaner simply couldn't, and that there must be a kind of continuity of rhythm in your relationship to the canvas by which the conscious manipulation, the throwing of paint and the continuation of conscious manipulation are all part of one process.

FB  I wouldn't like to exclude the idea that somebody could come in and do it as well or better. I wouldn't like to cancel out that it could happen; because I think it could happen. It might be different, it might be better, or it might be worse. Of course they wouldn't know what to do with it afterwards.

DS  Naturally. Now, on a day when, say, you're in form, do you find that, when your conscious activity is going well, the accidental activity will also be going well?

FB  Yes. And one of the things is, of course, that in one's conscious activity in painting – at any rate in oil painting, which is such a fluid and curious medium – often the tension will be completely changed by just the way a stroke of the brush goes on. It breeds another form that the form you're making can take. I mean, there are all sorts of things happening all the time, and it's difficult to distinguish between the conscious and the unconscious working, or the instinctive working, whichever you like to call it.

DS  And aren't the good days those days when areas open up which you hadn't predicted? Those are precisely what good days are, aren't they?

FB  Yes, of course.

DS  But then this does tend, I would say, to give the lie to the idea that the cleaner could get equally good results.

FB   The thing is that, if you were just going to leave the one piece of thrown paint, they might be able to, but, if you're going to manipulate, obviously not.

DS   But even apart from the manipulation.

FB   Well, hazard plays such odd tricks, one doesn't know.

DS   We've talked before about roulette and about the feeling one sometimes has at the table that one is kind of in tune with the wheel and can do nothing wrong. How does this relate to the painting process?

FB   Well, I'm sure there certainly is a very strong relationship. After all, Picasso once said: I don't need to play games of chance, I'm always working with it myself.

DS   Well, unlike the cleaner, the roulette wheel really is a machine. One might say that, while the roulette wheel really does work according to the laws of chance, somehow, when one is playing in an inspired way, it's as if it didn't – it's as if it were working according to certain laws which were not those of chance and that somehow you could get on the wave-length of the way it's working on that particular day.

FB   Well, that is one of those curious things that one doesn't know anything about. It's rather like when I did once make quite a lot of money, for me at any rate, playing roulette and I did actually think I could hear the numbers being called before they came up. But one can't say whether those particular things are in fact so-called extra-sensory perception or if they are really just a run of luck.

DS   And with the painting?

FB   Well, again, I don't think one really knows whether it's a run of luck or whether it's instinct working in your favour or whether it's instinct and consciousness and everything intermingling and working in your favour.

DS   Then isn't that what Frank Auerbach means when he says it's not really accident at all?

FB   It may be what he means, it may be what he means. I don't know with Frank, because he always wants to be contradictory with me.

DS   Perhaps he means that the operations you think of as random are more an inspired kind of letting-go and that the difference between these and the manipulation is one of degree rather than kind.

F B   I know that sometimes, when I've been working and things were going so badly, I've just taken a brush and put the paint anywhere, not knowing consciously what I was doing, and suddenly the thing has sometimes begun to work.

D S   That sounds awfully conclusive. What I think I've been trying to suggest is that accident is always present and control is always present and there's a tremendous overlap between the two.

F B   Yes, I think there is, I think that is so. And yet, what so-called chance gives you is quite different from what willed application of paint gives you. It has an inevitability very often which the willed putting-on of the paint doesn't give you.

D S   Is that because with the willed putting-on one kind of tightens up? Is that what illustration means? – a kind of caution, a lack of relaxation?

75 Detail from right-hand panel of *93*

F B   Well, illustration surely means just illustrating the

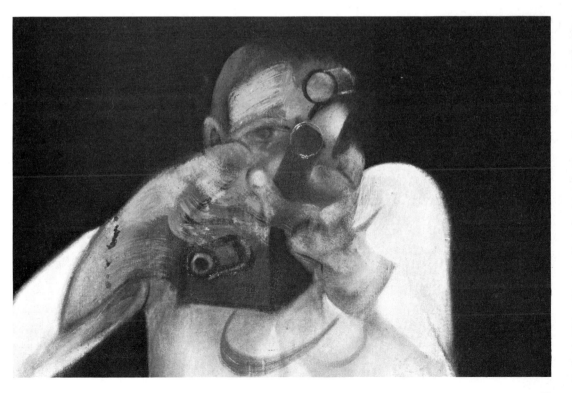

78 (Opposite) *Sleeping Figure* 1974

image before you, not inventing it. I don't know how I can say any more about it than what you know. Because, you see, it's impossible to talk about chance when you don't know what it is. When people like Frank say it isn't chance or accident or whatever you like to call it, in a way I know what they mean. And yet I don't know what they mean, because I don't think one can explain it. It would be like trying to explain the unconscious. It's also always hopeless talking about painting – one never does anything but talk around it – because, if you could explain your painting, you would be explaining your instincts.

DS   No, you can't explain your painting, and nobody can explain their own painting or any painting, but you can throw light on your painting.

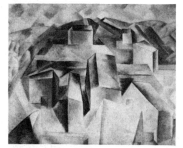

76 PICASSO *Houses on a Hill (Horta de San Juan)* 1909

FB   I don't know what it's about myself. I don't really know how these particular forms come about. I'm not by that suggesting that I'm inspired or gifted. I just don't know. I look at them – I look at them, probably, from an aesthetic point of view. I know what I want to do, but I don't know how to do it. And I look at them almost like a stranger, not knowing how these things have come about and why have these marks that have happened on the canvas evolved into these particular forms. And then, of course, I remember what I wanted to do and I do, of course, try then and push these irrational forms into what I originally wanted to do.

DS   I think that the best works of modern artists often give the impression that they were done when the artist was in a state of not knowing – for example, Picasso and Braque in those very late analytical-cubist pictures, where the whole thing seems totally inexplicable and one really can't believe that they knew what they were doing. They may have contructed a whole theoretical rationalization around it, and in the early analytical-cubist pictures it's fairly clear what is happening: you can more or less analyze the dislocations and the relationship of the forms to reality. But when you get to the very late analytical-cubist works, there's a totally mysterious relationship to reality which you can't begin to analyze, and you sense that the artist didn't know what he was doing, that he had a kind of rightness of instinct and that only instinct was operating, and that somehow he was working beyond reason.

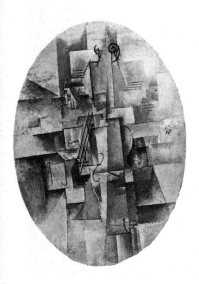

77 PICASSO *Still Life with a Violin* 1911–12

FB   Surely this is the cause of the difficulty of painting today – that it will only catch the mystery of reality if the

**100**

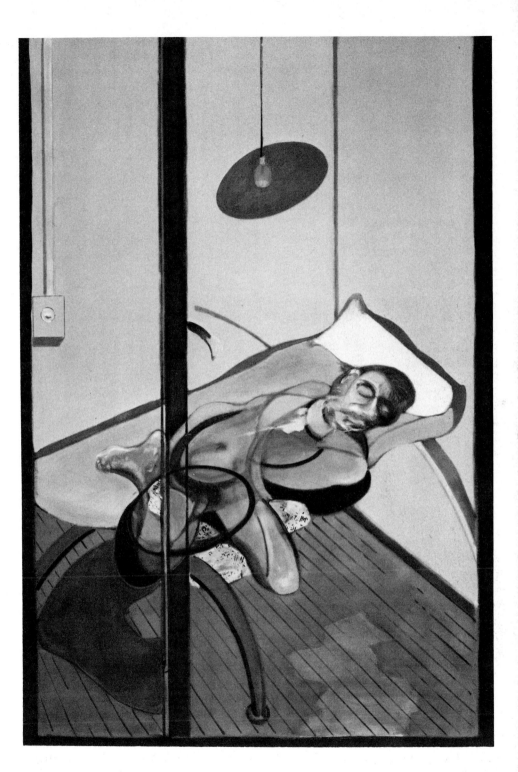

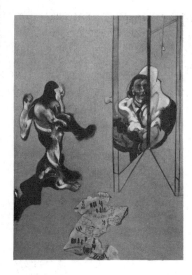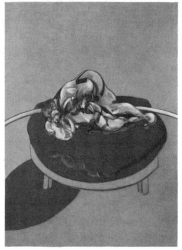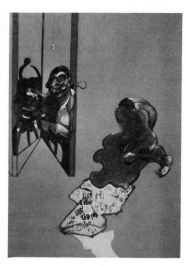

79 *Triptych – Studies from the Human Body* 1970

painter doesn't know how to do it. And he's carried along by his passion and he doesn't perhaps even know quite what these marks will make, and yet, in a funny way. . . . I don't know about the cubist painters, whether they knew what they wanted to do. As you say, with early analytical cubism you can just literally see the town on a hill and all that kind of thing – they've just been cubed up. But perhaps in the later ones Picasso knew what he wanted to do but didn't know how to bring it about. I don't know about that. I know that, in my case, I know what I want to do but don't know how to bring it about. And that's what I'm hoping accidents or chance or whatever you like to call it will bring about for me. So that it's a continuous thing between what may be called luck or hazard, intuition and the critical sense. Because it's only kept hold of by the critical sense, the criticism of your own instincts about how far this given form or accidental form crystallizes into what you want.

DS   When it has crystallized for you, do you know it immediately or do you need a few weeks or months to be sure?

FB   Well, if my work goes at all well, it goes very quickly. For instance, in the orange triptych of 1970 which you said that you quite liked, where the centre panel has two figures on a bed – well, I knew that I wanted to put two figures together on a bed, and I knew that I wanted them in a sense either to be copulating or buggering – whichever way you like to put it – but I didn't know how to do it so that it would have the strength of the sensation which I had about it. I

80 (Opposite) Centre panel of *79*

102

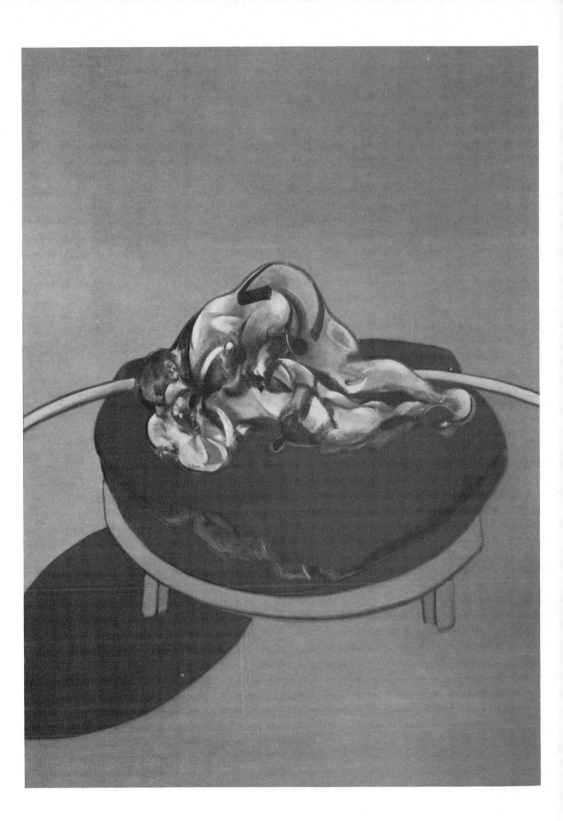

just had to leave it to chance to attempt to make an image. I wanted to make an image which coagulated this sensation of two people in some form of sexual act on the bed, but then I was left completely in the void and left absolutely to the haphazard marks which I make all the time. And then I worked on what's called the given form. And, if you look at the forms, they're extremely, in a sense, unrepresentational. One of the things I've always tried to analyze is why it is that, if the formation of the image that you want is done irrationally, it seems to come onto the nervous system much more strongly than if you knew how you could do it. Why is it possible to make the reality of an appearance more violently in this way than by doing it rationally? Perhaps it's that, if the making is more instinctive, the image is more immediate.

DS   Yet, along with this need to act freely and instinctively, there's also the need, as you said, for your critical sense to keep hold. I suppose the whole of art lies in this mysterious conjunction of being able to let go and yet being able to remain sufficiently apart to see where one has to stop.

FB   In my case, there's also another thing – that I really like very formal art, and I think, perhaps, as I tend to get older, I try and make it in a sense freer and yet more formal. And that again is a problem. But I think that what you say is, of course, the core of this thing. There's an extremely good lecture which Duchamp gave in 1958, I think, in Houston.

DS   I'll get it off the shelf. What about this? 'To all appearances, the artist acts like a mediumistic being who, from the labyrinth beyond time and space, seeks his way out to a clearing.'

FB   Where he's using 'medium', you use 'trance'.

DS   'If we give the attributes of a medium to the artist, we must then deny him the state of consciousness on the aesthetic plane about what he is doing or why he is doing it. All his decisions in the artistic execution of the work rest with pure intuition and cannot be translated into a self-analysis, spoken or written, or even thought out.' And later he says this: 'In the creative act, the artist goes from intention to realization through a chain of totally subjective reactions. His struggle towards the realization is a series of efforts, pains, satisfactions, refusals, decisions, which also cannot and must not be fully self-conscious, at least on the aesthetic plane.'

FB   Yes, they cannot be. It's not that they must not be. They cannot be.

DS   Does that help to disentangle what we've been talking about?

FB   Not exactly, not quite. Because there is a difference. Most of Duchamp is figurative, but I think he made sort of symbols of the figurative. And he made, in a sense, a sort of myth of the twentieth century, but in terms of making a shorthand of figuration. Well, now, what personally I would like to do would be, for instance, to make portraits which were portraits but came out of things which really had nothing to do with what is called the illustrational facts of the image; they would be made differently, and yet they would give the appearance. To me, the mystery of painting today is how can appearance be made. I know it can be illustrated, I know it can be photographed. But how can this thing be made so that you catch the mystery of appearance within the mystery of the making? It's an illogical method of making, an illogical way of attempting to make what one hopes will be a logical outcome – in the sense that one hopes one will be able to suddenly make the thing there in a totally illogical way but that it will be totally real and, in the case of a portrait, recognizable as the person.

DS   Could one put it like this? – that you're trying to make an image of appearance that is conditioned as little as possible by the accepted standards of what appearance is.

FB   That's a very good way of putting it. There's a further step to that: the whole questioning of what appearance is. There are standards set up as to what appearance is or should be, but there's no doubt that the ways appearance can be made are very mysterious ways, because one knows that by some accidental brushmarks suddenly appearance comes in with a vividness that no accepted way of doing it would have brought about. I'm always trying through chance or accident to find a way by which appearance can be there but remade out of other shapes.

DS   And the otherness of those shapes is crucial.

FB   It is. Because, if the thing seems to come off at all, it comes off because of a kind of darkness which the otherness

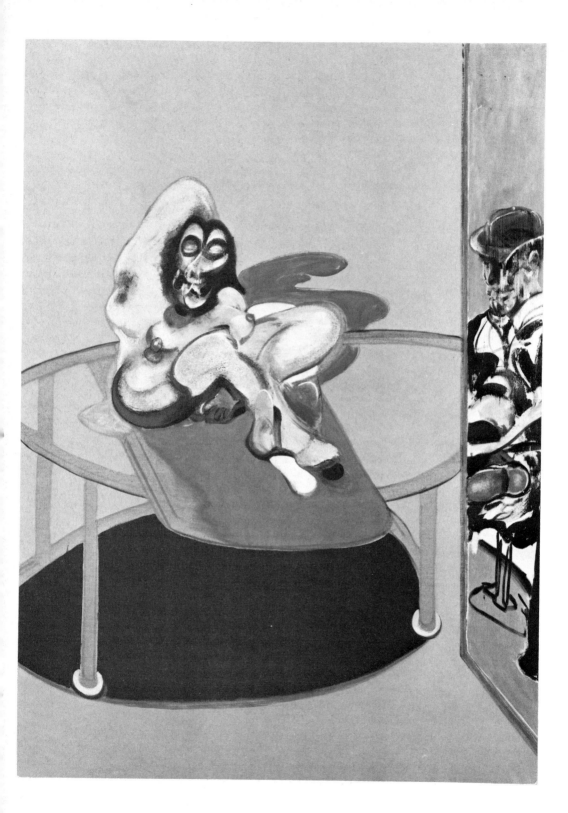

of the shape which isn't known, as it were, conveys to it. For instance, one could make a mouth in a way – I mean, it comes about sometimes, one doesn't know how – I mean you could draw the mouth right across the face as though it was almost like the opening of the whole head, and yet it could be like the mouth. But, in trying to do a portrait, my ideal would really be just to pick up a handful of paint and throw it at the canvas and hope that the portrait was there.

DS   I can see why you would want the painting to look as if it had come about in that way, but do you mean you actually want to do that?

FB   Well, I've tried often enough. But it's never worked that way. I think I would like it to happen that way because, as you know perfectly well, if you have somebody painting your room, when he puts the first brushstroke on the wall, it's much more exciting than the finished wall. And, although I may use, or appear to use, traditional methods, I want those methods to work for me in a very different way to that in which they have worked before or for which they were originally formed. I'm not attempting to use what's called avant-garde techniques. Most people this century who have had anything to do with the avant garde have wanted to create a new technique, and I never have myself. Perhaps I have nothing to do with the avant garde. But I've never felt it at all necessary to try and create an absolutely specialized technique. I think the only man who didn't limit himself tremendously by trying to change the technique was Duchamp, who did it enormously successfully. But, although I may use what's called the techniques that have been handed down, I'm trying to make out of them something that is radically different to what those techniques have made before.

DS   Why do you want it to be radically different?

FB   Because I think my sensibility is radically different, and, if I work as closely as I can to my own sensibility, there is a possibility that the image will have a greater reality.

DS   And do you still have that obsession you used to talk about having with doing the one perfect image?

FB   No, I don't now. I suppose, as I get older, I feel I want to cover wider areas. I don't think that I have that other feeling any longer – perhaps because I hope to go on painting until I die and, of course, if you did the one absolutely perfect image, you would never do anything more. □ □ □

4

DS  I've found that quite a number of the paintings you've done in the last three or four years – especially paintings of the nude – have tended to remind me that for some time now you've been talking about wanting to do sculpture. Do you yourself feel that thinking about doing sculpture has had any effect on the way you've been painting?

FB  Yes, I think it's quite possible. Because for several years now I've been very much thinking about sculpture, though I haven't ever yet done it, because each time I want to do it I get the feeling that perhaps I could do it better in painting. But now I have decided to make a series of paintings of the sculptures in my mind and see how they come out as paintings. And then I might actually start on sculpture.

DS  Can you give any sort of description of sculptures that you've thought of doing?

FB  I've thought about sculptures on a kind of armature, a very large armature made so that the sculpture could slide along it and people could even alter the position of the sculpture as they wanted. The armature would not be as important as the image, but it would be there to set it off, as I have very often used an armature to set off the image in paintings. I've felt that in sculpture I would perhaps be able to do it more poignantly.

DS  Would the armature be anything like the sorts of rail which you've sometimes used in paintings – for instance,

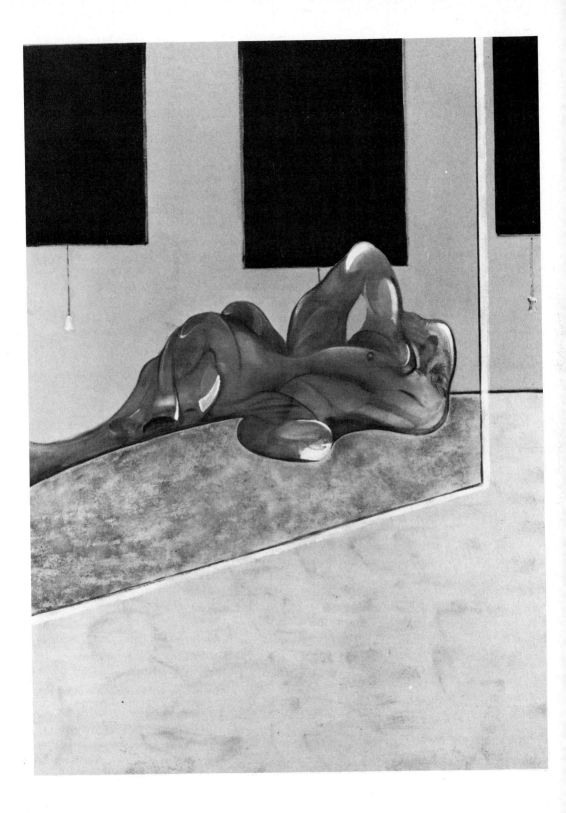

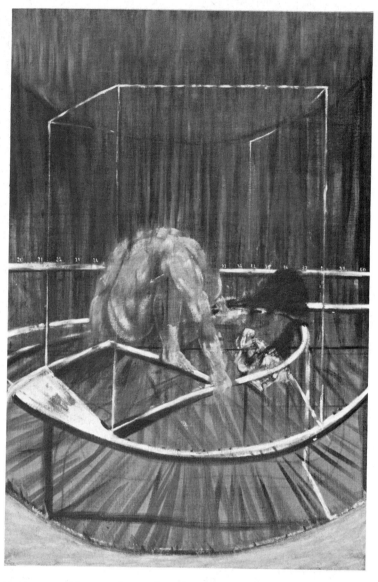

83 *Study for Crouching Nude* 1952

84 (Opposite) *After Muybridge –*
*Woman Emptying Bowl of Water*
*and Paralytic Child on All Fours*
1965

that crouching male nude of 1952 or the picture done in 1965 with a woman and a child taken from Muybridge?

FB   Yes. I've thought of the rail in very highly-polished steel and that it would be slotted so that the image could be screwed into place in different positions.

DS   Have you visualized the colours and textures of the images?

FB   I would have to talk to somebody who technically understood sculpture much more than I do, but I myself have

**110**

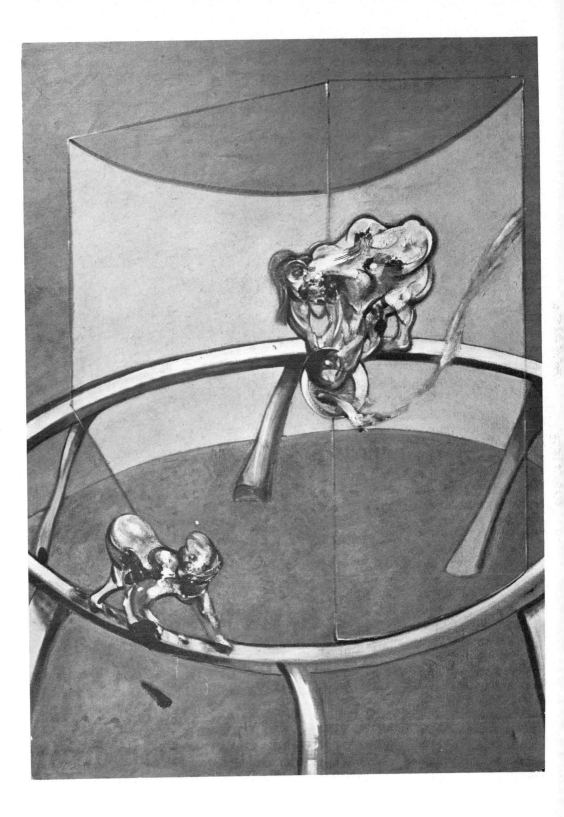

thought they should be cast in a very thin bronze – not in some kind of plastic, because I would want them to have the weight of bronze – and I've wanted to throw over them a coat of flesh-coloured whitewash, so that they'd look as though they had been dipped into an ordinary kind of white-wash, with the sort of texture of sand and lime that you get. So that you would have the feeling of this flesh and this highly-polished steel.

DS   And what sort of scale have you seen them as having?

FB   I've seen the armature as a very large space, like a street, and the images as comparatively small in relation to the space. The images would be naked figures, but not literal naked figures; I've seen them as very formal images of figures in different attitudes, either single or coupled. Whether I do them or not, I shall certainly try and do them in painting, and I hope I shall be able to do them in sculpture if they come off at all in the paintings. I shall probably do them in painting on the reverse side of the canvas, which might give some illusion of how they might look if they were left in space.

DS   Of course, the *Three Studies for Figures at the Base of a Crucifixion* of 1944 (*3*) are clearly defined plastic forms which could almost be copied in sculpture.

FB   Well, I thought of them as the Eumenides, and at the time I saw the whole Crucifixion in which these would be there instead of the usual figures at the base of the cross. And I was going to put these on an armature around the cross, which itself was going to be raised, and the image on the cross was to be in the centre with these things arranged around it. But I never did that; I just left these as attempts.

DS   There's a very recent painting with a figure of a man seated in a room facing a window and outside the window a kind of phantasmal figure which is once more, you've said, a representation of the Eumenides. And that phantasm, it seems to me, is about as purely and simply sculptural as the 1944 Eumenides. But it's the figure of the man in this painting, or that reclining figure with window-blinds in the background which you painted three years ago (*82*) that strike me as typical of the way the figures tend to be sculptural now. It's more complex now, because now, when you create a defined sculptural form, it's qualified through nuances in the paint which create many suggestions and ambiguities. Neverthe-less, those figures have a very emphatic plasticity.

85 (Opposite) *Seated Figure* 1974

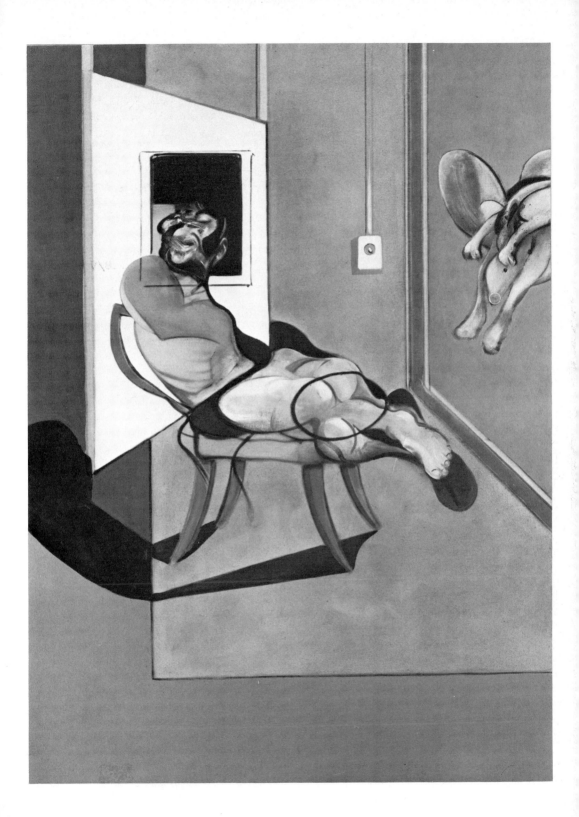

FB Well, I would like now – and I suppose it's through thinking about sculpture – I would like, quite apart from the attempt to do sculpture, to make the painting itself very much more sculptural. I do see in these images the way in which the mouth, the eyes, the ears could be used in painting so that they were there in a totally irrational way but a more realistic way, but I haven't come round yet to seeing quite how that could be done in sculpture. I might be able to come round to it. I do see all the time images that keep on coming up which are more and more formal and more and more based upon the human body, yet taken further from it in imagery. And I would like to make the portraits more sculptural, because I think it is possible to make a thing both a great image and a great portrait.

DS It's very interesting that you associate the idea of the great image with sculpture. Perhaps this goes back to your love of Egyptian sculpture?

FB Well, it's possible. I think that perhaps the greatest images that man has so far made have been in sculpture. I'm thinking of some of the great Egyptian sculpture, of course, and Greek sculpture too. For instance, the Elgin Marbles in the British Museum are always very important to me, but I don't know if they're important because they're fragments, and whether if one had seen the whole image they would seem as poignant as they seem as fragments. And I've always thought about Michelangelo; he's always been deeply important in my way of thinking about form. But although I have this profound admiration for all his work, the work that I like most of all is the drawings. For me he is one of the very greatest draughtsmen, if not the greatest.

DS I've often suspected, since as far back as 1950, that, with many of your nude figures, certain Michelangelo images had been there in the back of your mind at least, as proto-types of the male figure. Do you think this has been the case?

FB Actually, Michelangelo and Muybridge are mixed up in my mind together, and so I perhaps could learn about positions from Muybridge and learn about the ampleness, the grandeur of form from Michelangelo, and it would be very difficult for me to disentangle the influence of Muybridge and the influence of Michelangelo. But, of course, as most of my figures are taken from the male nude, I am sure that I have been influenced by the fact that Michelangelo made the most voluptuous male nudes in the plastic arts.

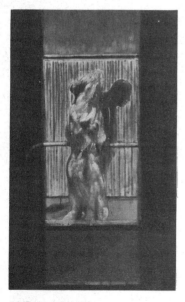

86 *Painting* 1950

87 (Opposite) MICHELANGELO
Sheet of studies 1511 and 1513

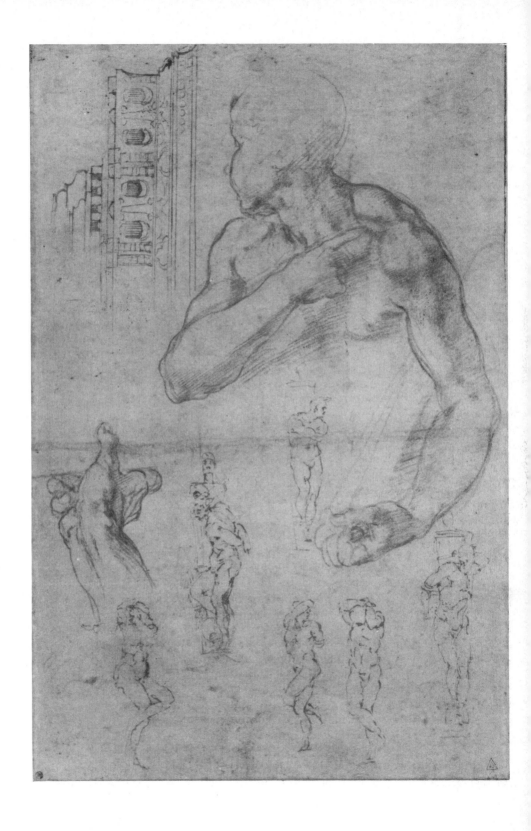

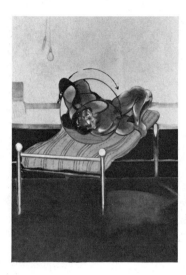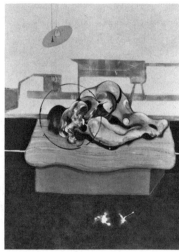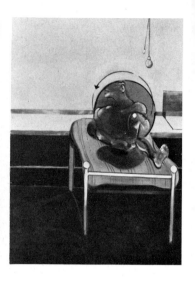

88 *Three Studies of Figures on Beds*
1972

90 (Opposite) Centre panel of *88*

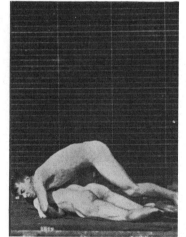

89 MUYBRIDGE Photograph from
*The Human Figure in Motion* 1887

DS  Do you think that certain Michelangelo images of figures entwined have had an influence on your coupled figures?

FB  Well, these have very often been taken from the Muybridge wrestlers – some of which appear, unless you look at them under a microscope, to be in some form of sexual embrace. Actually, I've often used the wrestlers in painting single figures, because I find that the two figures together have a thickness that gives overtones which the photographs of single figures don't have. But I don't only look at Muybridge photographs of the figure. I look all the time at photographs in magazines of footballers and boxers and all that kind of thing – especially boxers. And I also look at animal photographs all the time. Because animal movement and human movement are continually linked in my imagery of human movement.

DS  And are the nudes, at the same time, closely related to the appearance of specific people? Are they to some extent portraits of bodies?

FB  Well, it's a complicated thing. I very often think of people's bodies that I've known, I think of the contours of those bodies that have particularly affected me, but then they're grafted very often onto Muybridge's bodies. I manipulate the Muybridge bodies into the form of the bodies I have known. But, of course, in my case, with this disruption all the time of the image – or distortion, or whatever you

**116**

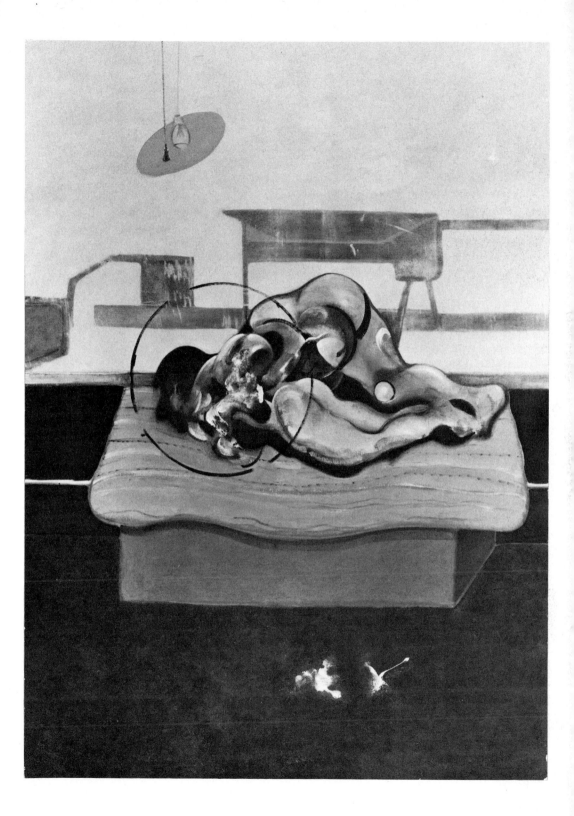

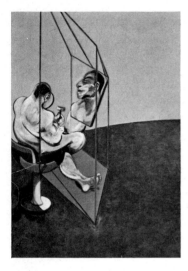 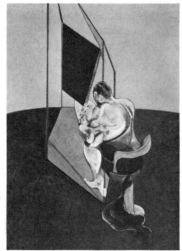 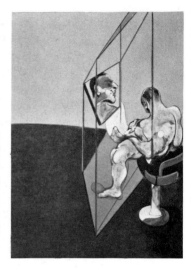

91 *Three Studies of the Male Back* 1970

92 (Opposite) Left-hand panel of *91*

like to call it – it's an elliptical way of coming to the appearance of that particular body. And the way I try to bring appearance about makes one question all the time what appearance is at all. The longer you work, the more the mystery deepens of what appearance is, or how can what is called appearance be made in another medium. And it needs a sort of moment of magic to coagulate colour and form so that it gets the equivalent of appearance, the appearance that you see at any moment, because so-called appearance is only riveted for one moment as that appearance. In a second you may blink your eyes or turn your head slightly, and you look again and the appearance has changed. I mean, appearance is like a continuously floating thing. And, of course, in sculpture the problem is perhaps even more poignant because the material which you would be working in is not as fluid as oil paint and it would add another difficulty. But then an added difficulty often is what makes the solving of a thing deeper. Because of the difficulty in doing it.

DS   It seems to me that in your painting you've confronted an immense and extraordinary kind of difficulty which possibly relates to your desire that the form should be at once very precise and very ambiguous. In that triptych of 1944 (*3*) you used a hard bright ground for very precisely and simply displayed forms, carved-out forms, as it were, and that was entirely consistent. Then the handling of the forms became *malerisch*, and with this the background became softer, more tonal, often curtained, and all that was entirely consistent. But then you got rid of the curtains; you came to

118

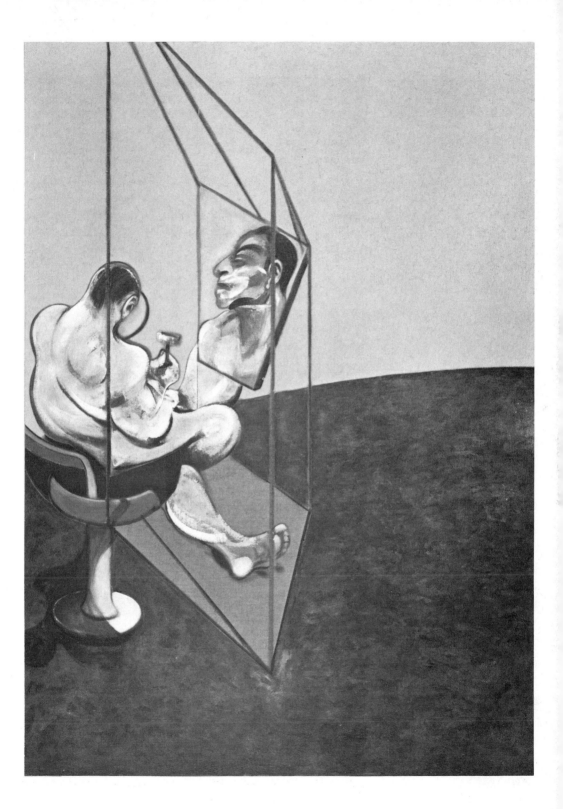

combine a *malerisch* handling of the form – and with the paint getting more and more scrambled – with a hard, flat, bright ground, so that you violently juxtapose two opposite conventions.

FB   Well, I've increasingly wanted to make the images simpler and more complicated. And for this to work, it can work more starkly if the background is very united and clear. I think that probably is why I have used a very clear background against which the image can articulate itself.

DS   I don't think I can think of any other painter who has tried to resolve such a contradiction between a *malerisch* image and a vivid, uninflected ground.

FB   Well, that may be because I hate a homely atmosphere, and I always feel that *malerisch* painting has too homely a background. I would like the intimacy of the image against a very stark background. I want to isolate the image and take it away from the interior and the home. □ □ □


DS   Going back over those long discussions about chance or accident, I've been especially struck by two of the thoughts that recur. One is your dislike of paintings looking what you call 'chancy'. And the other is your belief that things which come about by chance are more likely to seem to have a certain inevitability than things which come about by will. Can you say why you feel that an image will tend to look more inevitable the more it comes about by accident?

FB   It hasn't been interfered with. And it seems to be fresher. The hinges of form come about by chance seem to be more organic and to work more inevitably.

DS   Lack of interference – is that the clue?

FB   Yes. The will has been subdued by the instinct.

DS   You're saying that, in allowing chance to work, one allows the deeper levels of the personality to come across?

FB   I certainly am trying to say that. But I'm also trying to say that they come over inevitably – they come over without the brain interfering with the inevitability of an image. It seems to come straight out of what we choose to call the unconscious with the foam of the unconscious locked around it – which is its freshness.

DS   Now, you often say that the accidents which are most fruitful tend to happen at the time of greatest despair about how to go on with a painting. On the other hand, when I once asked you whether, on days when conscious operations were going well, chance operations would also be likely to be going well, you said they would. Of course that statement isn't incompatible with the others, but could you enlarge?

FB   Well, there are certain days when you start working and the work seems to flow out of you quite easily, but that doesn't often happen and doesn't last for long. And I don't know that it's necessarily any better than when something happens out of your frustration and despair. I think· that, quite possibly, when things are going badly you will be freer with the way you mess up by just putting paint through the images that you've been making, and you do it with a greater abandon than if things have been working for you. And therefore I think, perhaps, that despair is more helpful, because out of despair you may find yourself making the image in a more radical way by taking greater risks.

DS   You've told me that half of your painting activity is disrupting what you can do easily. What is it you can do easily and want to disrupt?

FB   I can quite easily sit down and make what is called a literal portrait of you. So what I'm disrupting all the time is this literalness, because I find it uninteresting.

DS   And I take it that marks made with the brush can be just as disruptive as operations like throwing paint or applying a rag.

FB   Oh certainly. With oil paint being so fluid, the image is changing all the time while you're working. One thing either builds on another or destroys the other. You see, I don't think that generally people really understand how mysterious, in a way, the actual manipulation of oil paint is. Because moving – even unconsciously moving – the brush one way rather than the other will completely alter the implications of the image. But you could only see it if it happened before you. I mean, it's in the way that one end of the brush may be filled with another colour and the pressing of the brush, by accident, makes a mark which gives a resonance to the other marks; and this leads on to a further development of the image. It's really a continuous question of the fight between accident and criticism. Because what I call accident may

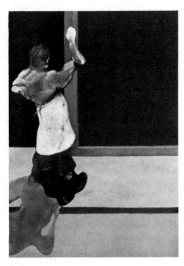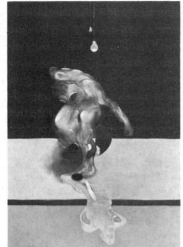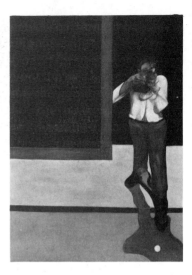

93 *Triptych – March 1974*

give you some mark that seems to be more real, truer to the image than another one, but it's only your critical sense that can select it. So that your critical faculty is going on at the same time as the sort of half-unconscious manipulation – or very unconscious, generally, if it works at all.

DS   Of course, trusting to chance seems to be something that pervades the whole way you live your life. For one thing, it's very obvious in your attitude to money. At the time I first knew you, you didn't get a lot of money for a painting but, even then, the moment you sold one you'd be buying champagne and caviar for everyone in sight. You never held back. You've always seemed free of prudence.

FB   Well, that's because of my greed. I'm greedy for life; and I'm greedy as an artist. I'm greedy for what I hope chance can give me far beyond anything that I can calculate logically. And it's partly my greed that has made me what's called live by chance – greed for food, for drink, for being with the people one likes, for the excitement of things happening. So the same thing applies to one's work. I nevertheless, when I cross the road, do look both ways. Because, with the greed for life, I don't play it in the way that I also want to be killed, as some people do. Because life is so short and, while I can move and see and feel, I want life to go on existing.

DS   Your taste for roulette doesn't, as it were, extend to Russian roulette.

94 (Opposite) Centre panel of *93*

FB   No. Because to do what I want to do would mean, if

122

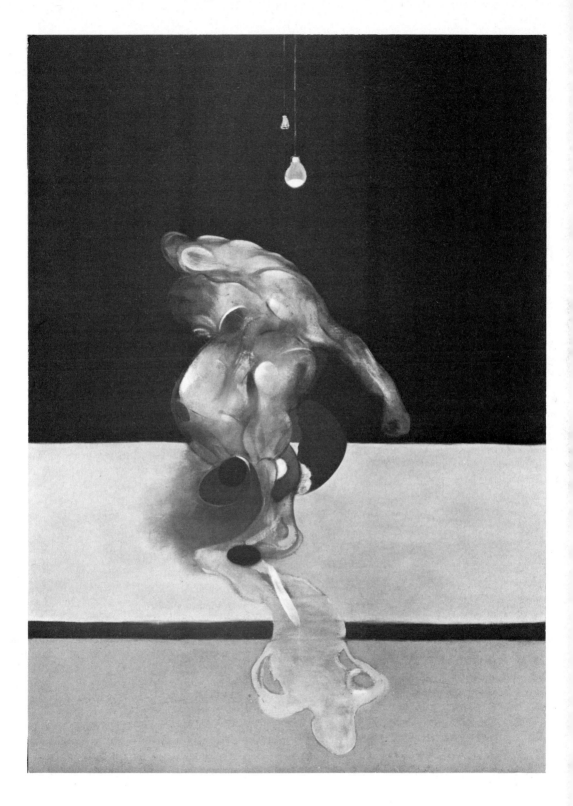

possible, living. Whereas the other day somebody was telling me about De Staël – that Russian roulette was an obsession with him and that very often he would drive round the corniche at night at tremendous speed on the wrong side of the road, purposely to see whether he could avoid the thing or not avoid it. I do know how he's supposed to have died; that out of despair he committed suicide. But for me the idea of Russian roulette would be futile. Also, I haven't got that kind of what's called bravery. I'm sure physical danger actually can be very exhilarating. But I think I'm too much of a coward to court it myself. And also, as I want to go on living, as I want to make my work better, out of vanity, you may say, I have got to live, I've got to exist.

DS   When you didn't have much money but were spending it as you did, were you ever left destitute for a time? Or did something always come to the rescue?

FB   Well, I have often manipulated things so that they should come to my rescue. I think I'm one of those people who have a gift for always getting by somehow. Even if it's a case of stealing or something like that, I don't feel any moral thing against it. I suppose that's an extremely egocentric attitude. It would be a nuisance to be caught and put in prison, but I don't have any feeling about stealing. Now that I earn money, it would be a kind of stupid luxury to go out and steal. But when I had no money, I think I often used to take what I could get.

DS   I have the impression that following one's impulses and accepting the consequences and ignoring security isn't just the way you yourself behave; it's also a prejudice that governs your view of society. I mean that you talk as if the concept of the welfare state, with its guarantee of certain kinds of security, seems to you a sort of perversion of life.

FB   Well, I think that being nursed by the state from the cradle to the grave would bring such a boredom to life. But in saying that, it may be something to do with that I have never had the morality of poverty. And therefore I can't think of anything more boring than that everything was looked after for you from your birth to your death. But people seem to expect that and think it is their right. I think that, if people have that attitude to life, it curtails – I believe this, I cannot prove it – the creative instinct. It would be difficult to understand why. But I never believe one should have any security and never expect to keep any.

DS  You feel that it's, as I said, a kind of perversion of life and its possibilities that people should seek security?

FB  Well, it's the opposite of the despair about life and the despair about existence. After all, as existence in a way is so banal, you may as well try and make a kind of grandeur of it rather than be nursed to oblivion.

DS  Obviously what politics is basically about is the conflict between individual freedom and social justice, and you clearly think of individual freedom as something far more important than social justice. You don't get disturbed when you see social injustice?

FB  I think it's the texture of life. I know that you can say that all life is completely artificial, but I think that what is called social justice makes it more pointlessly artificial.

DS  And you're not disturbed by the kinds of suffering which are endured by some people as a result of social injustice?

FB  No. When you say they don't disturb me, I'm in a way very conscious of them. But I think, as I live in a country where there has been a certain amount of wealth, it's difficult to talk about a country where there has always been extreme poverty. And it's quite possible that people could be helped in extremely poor countries to exist on a plane where it was possible for them to escape from their hunger and their general despair. But I'm not upset by the fact that people do suffer, because I think the suffering of people and the differences between people are what have made great art, and not egalitarianism.

DS  You're saying, then, that the thing by which a society is to be judged is its potential for creating great art, rather than something like the greatest happiness of the greatest number?

FB  Who remembers or cares about a happy society? After hundreds of years or so, all they think about is what a society has left. I suppose it's possible that a society may arise which is so perfect that it will be remembered for the perfection of its equality. But that hasn't yet arisen, and so far one remembers a society for what it has created. □ □ □

**5**

FB   I think that in our previous discussions, when we've talked about the possibility of making appearance out of something which was not illustration, I've over-talked about it. Because, in spite of theoretically longing for the image to be made up of irrational marks, inevitably illustration has to come into it to make certain parts of the head and face which, if one left them out, one would then only be making an abstract design. I think what I very often have talked about has been perhaps a particular theory of mine which is impossible to achieve. Of course one does put in such things as ears and eyes. But then one would like to put them in as irrationally as possible. And the only reason for this irrationality is that, if it does come about, it brings the force of the image over very much more strongly than if one just sat down and illustrated the appearance, which of course millions of art students all over the world can do. But I'm quite prepared to believe that mine is a really far-out and impossible theory.

DS   Nevertheless, it's obviously of great importance for you to think in those terms.

FB   Certainly. It's one of the reasons that I go on painting, because it haunts me so much.

DS   When you come to think of it, this is very much, in one form or another, an aim that artists often feel – to make the thing unlike yet miraculously like. It's taken many forms, this idea of transforming the material very radically in order to make it more like itself. In one way or another it's a very common aim in art.

95 (Opposite) Left-hand panel of *61*

126

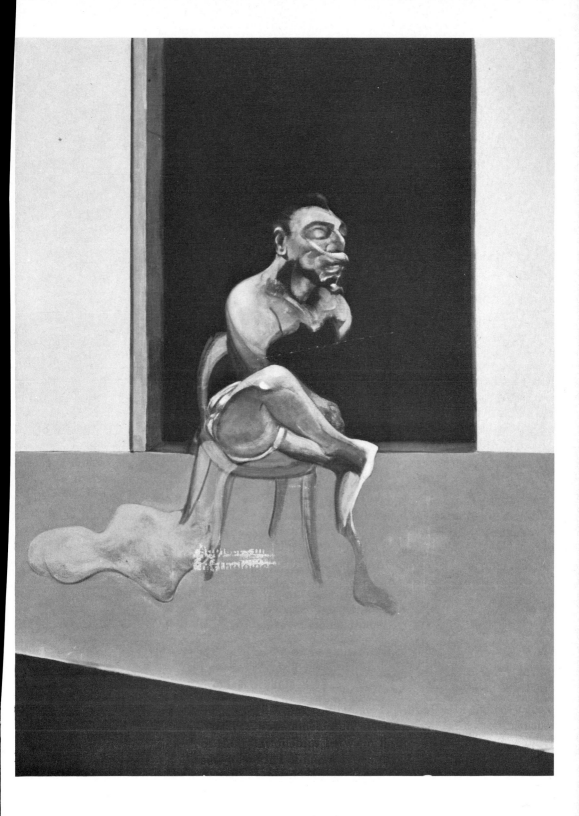

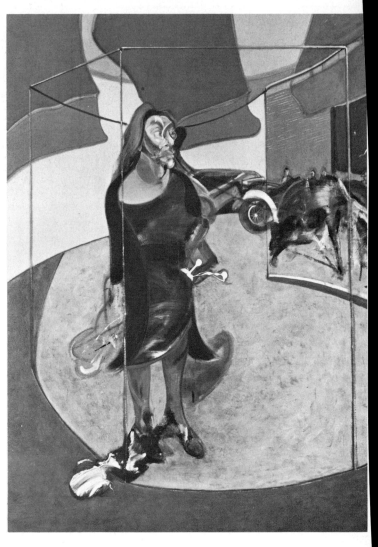

96 *Portrait of Isabel Rawsthorne
Standing in a Street in Soho* 1967

FB It's a common aim because it's almost an aim of creating magic if you could bring it about.

DS Looking at, say, that portrait you like of Isabel in the street, isn't it really a successful interlocking of clearly illustrational marks with highly suggestive irrational marks, which has some marks serving one purpose and other marks the other purpose?

FB Yes, it's certainly a mixture of the two, as you say.

DS Is it really possible with something as specific as a portrait for it to be anything else?

128

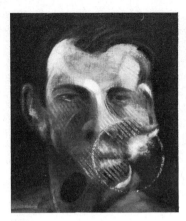 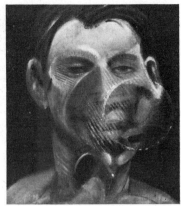 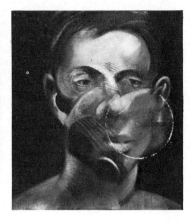

97 *Three Studies for a Portrait*
1975

FB Until somebody solves it, it won't be possible.

DS Do you sometimes find in working on a portrait that, when it's developing in such a way that the paint is very alive and strong, at the same time you're tending to lose the likeness of the specific person?

FB More often than not that does happen.

DS Do you feel you want to pull it back by strengthening some illustrational component?

FB No, I think you just lose it. It would be interesting to photograph these things all the time as you go along, because they're changing every moment, so that you'd be able to see what you'd lost and what you'd gained.

DS You've painted a great many self-portraits lately, haven't you, many more than before?

FB I've done a lot of self-portraits, really because people have been dying around me like flies and I've had nobody else left to paint but myself. Well, now I'm glad to say that two people, very good-looking, have turned up, both of whom I've known in the past. They're both very good subjects. I loathe my own face, and I've done self-portraits because I've had nobody else to do. But now I shall give up doing self-portraits.

DS You don't like to go on painting portraits of people after they're dead?

FB It seems a bit mad painting portraits of dead people. After all, you know that, if they haven't been – what's it called? – incinerated, they've rotted away; their flesh has

**129**

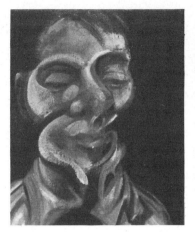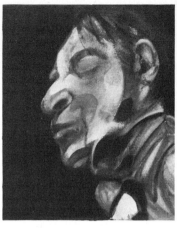

98 *Two Studies for Self-Portrait*
1972

rotted away, and once they're dead you have your memory of them but you haven't got them. I'm against incineration, because I think that in thousands of years' time, if the world exists at all, it will be a bore if there's nobody to dig up.

DS   When you're painting a portrait, are you at all conscious of trying to say something about your feelings in regard to the model or about what the model might be feeling, or are you only thinking about their appearance?

FB   Every form that you make has an implication, so that, when you are painting somebody, you know that you are, of course, trying to get near not only to their appearance but also to the way they have affected you, because every shape has an implication.

DS   An emotional implication?

FB   Yes.

DS   Are you conscious of that implication as you make it?

FB   Yes.

DS   That it might be aggressive, might be tender, and so forth?

FB   Yes.

DS   In painting self-portraits, is there a radical difference in approach from the one used when painting other people?

FB   No. Except that I like painting good-looking people because I like good bone structure. I loathe my own face, but

**130**

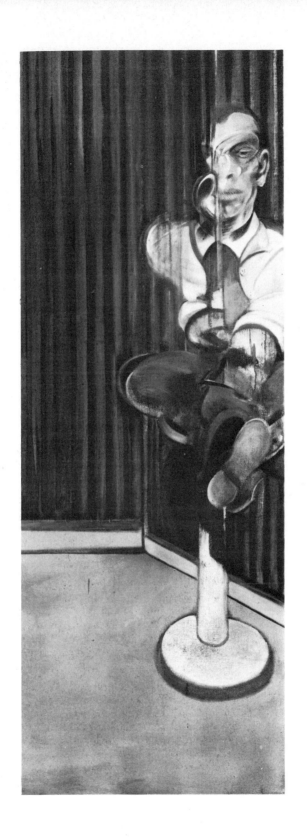

99 *Portrait of a Dwarf* 1975

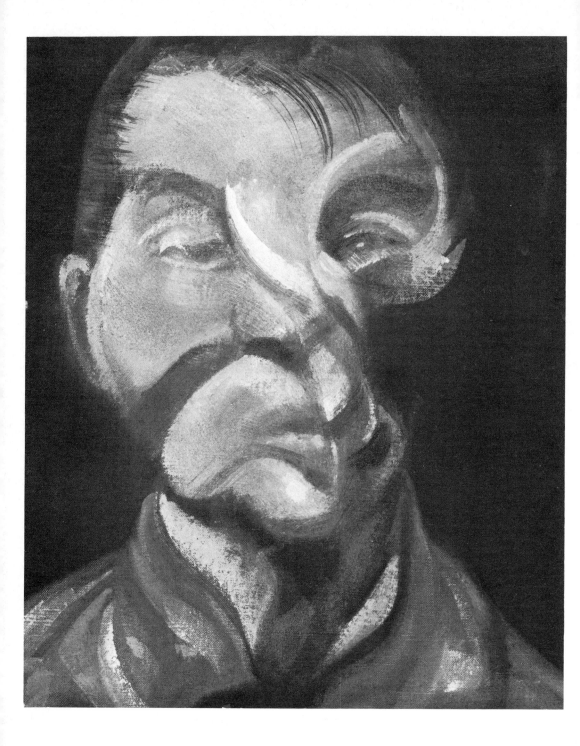

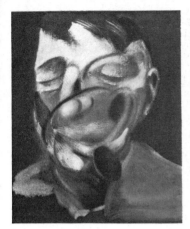 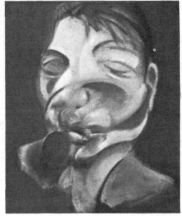 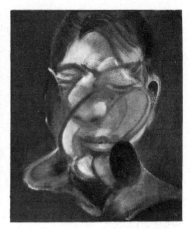

101 *Three Studies for a Self-Portrait* 1974

I go on painting it only because I haven't got any other people to do. It's true to say. . . . One of the nicest things that Cocteau said was: 'Each day in the mirror I watch death at work.' This is what one does oneself.

DS   At what age did you come to realize that death was going to happen to you too?

FB   I realized when I was seventeen. I remember it very, very clearly. I remember looking at a dog-shit on the pavement and I suddenly realized, there it is – this is what life is like. Strangely enough, it tormented me for months, till I came to, as it were, accept that here you are, existing for a second, brushed off like flies on the wall.

DS   You often quote Gloucester's lines, 'As flies to wanton boys are we to the gods;/ They kill us for their sport.' I've not heard you quote Edgar's lines, 'The gods are just, and of our pleasant vices/ Make instruments to plague us.' I take it that the first statement is the one with which you would tend to identify your own view of life.

FB   I think of life as meaningless; but we give it meaning during our own existence. We create certain attitudes which give it a meaning while we exist, though they in themselves are meaningless, really.

DS   A meaning in what sense?

FB   A way of existing from day to day.

DS   A purpose?

100 (Opposite) *Self-Portrait* 1972   FB   A purpose for nothing.

DS  So that, in spite of the sense that life is ultimately futile, nevertheless one finds the energy to do something which one believes in.

FB  Exactly. But believes in for nothing – but believes in. I know it's a contradiction in terms; it's nevertheless how it is. Because we are born and we die, but in between we give this purposeless existence a meaning by our drives.

DS  You have, of course, a very positive distaste for all forms of religion – as much for what you call modern mysticism as for Christianity – so I don't know how you feel about this, but for me the sort of shallow hedonism, the just wanting to have a good time, by which most people seem to live now, is a way to make life utterly boring.

FB  I absolutely agree with you. I think that most people who have religious beliefs, who have the fear of God, are much more interesting than people who just live a kind of hedonistic and drifting life. On the other hand, I can't help admiring but despising them, living by a total falseness, which I think they are living by with their religious views. But, after all, the only thing that makes anybody interesting is their dedication, and when there was religion they could at least be dedicated to their religion, which was something. But I do think that, if you can find a person totally without belief, but totally dedicated to futility, then you will find the more exciting person. ▢ ▢ ▢


DS  You said to me once that you can often sit and daydream and imagine rooms full of paintings that fall into your mind like slides. I'd like to know more about the extent to which you can visualize a painting before you start working on it.

FB  Well, it's certainly true that I can daydream for hours and pictures fall in just like slides. But it doesn't mean that the pictures that I finally end up with have anything to do with the paintings that dropped into my mind. Because what I see is a marvellous painting. But how are you going to make it? And, of course, as I don't know how to make it, I rely then on chance and accident making it for me.

DS  But what is it you see when you daydream?

FB  I see extraordinarily beautiful paintings.

102 (Opposite) *Self-Portrait* 1973    DS  They have the lay-out of the painting you actually do?

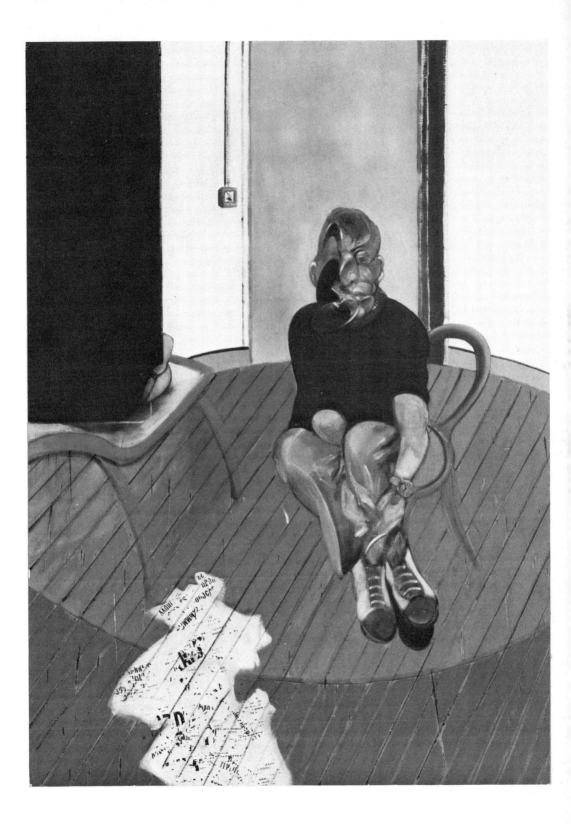

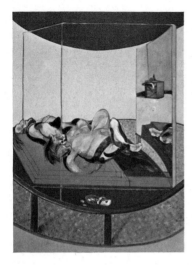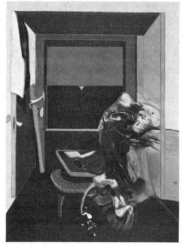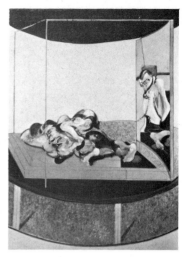

103 *Triptych – inspired by T.S. Eliot's poem 'Sweeney Agonistes'* 1967

FB To some extent, yes. But one has to start somewhere. Mind you, it's not the same thing with portraits. I don't find that portraits drop in the same way, because I find that portraits are even more accidental than the other types of paintings I do. Many things fall in which I've never been able to use. I don't think it's such a peculiar thing. I think it happens to every artist that things just drop in like slides.

DS To take an example, what about the *Sweeney Agonistes* triptych, which is a very complex composition that's also unlike any of the others, besides having a particular literary source of inspiration? How far was the composition foreseen?

FB I think in the *Sweeney Agonistes* I only knew that I wanted the central panel to be a panel without a figure.

DS You didn't know beforehand what was to happen in the outer panels?

FB I knew I wanted them to be figures; I didn't really know how those figures would work.

DS In the canvas of a seated figure with the Eumenides outside the window (*85*), did you foresee doing the Eumenides or was that an afterthought?

FB That was an afterthought. And in the one I did at about the same time, of a figure lying on a bed (*78*), I didn't in the first place intend to enclose it within those doors, and that came as an afterthought. I don't really think my pictures out, you know; I think of the disposition of the forms and then I watch the forms form themselves.

104 (Opposite) Centre panel of *103*

136

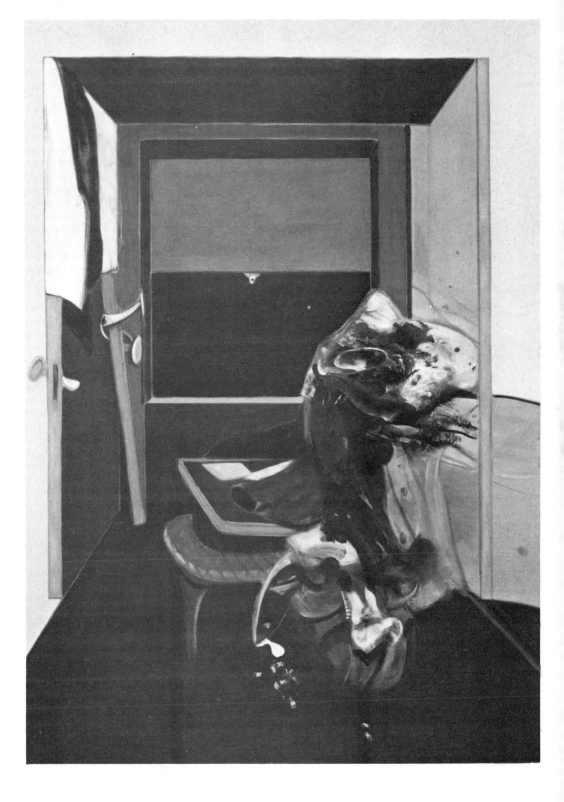

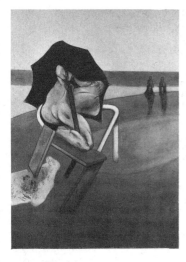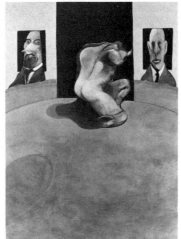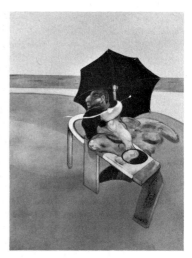

105 *Triptych 1974–77*

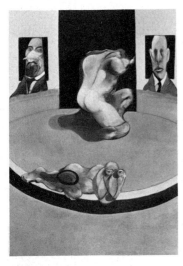

106 First state of centre panel of *105* 1974

107 (Opposite) Centre panel of *105* 1977

DS  In the beach triptych, were the horses and riders an afterthought?

FB  They were certainly an afterthought, yes. I felt that I just wanted that distance and movement and so on.

DS  And the screens with images of heads?

FB  Those are images I'd often thought about.

DS  Those you foresaw, then?

FB  Yes. I didn't foresee how the central figure would come out.

DS  You didn't know there was going to be a nude between the screens?

FB  Yes, but I didn't know how it was going to come out.

DS  You didn't know it was going to be a figure from the back?

FB  No.

DS  And the sort of semi-human figure down in front, was that foreseen?

FB  No, that wasn't foreseen.

DS  And the umbrellas?

FB  I didn't foresee those. This was a very unforeseen painting.

138

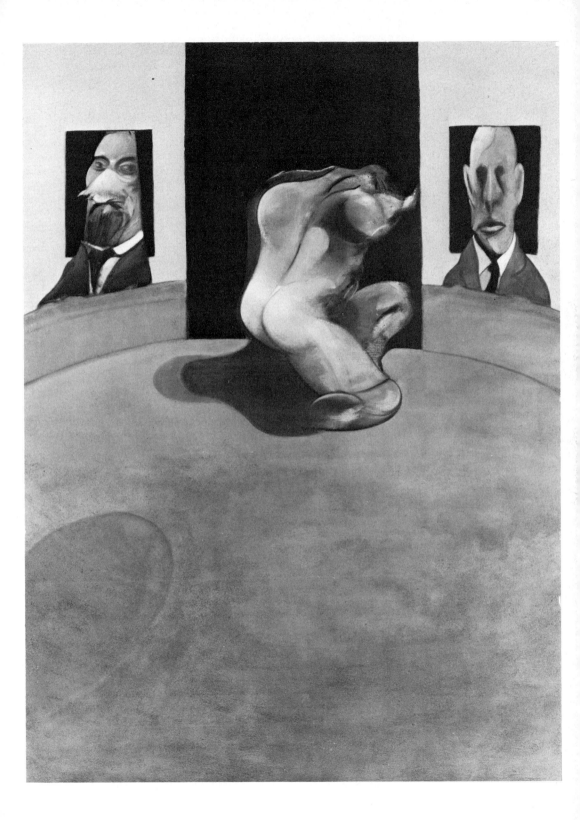

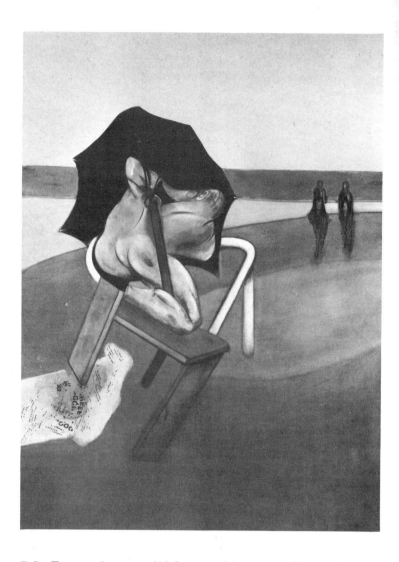

108 Left-hand panel of *105*

DS   Except that you did foresee this extraordinary element of the two heads on screens. Was it in order to do them that you started on this particular triptych?

FB   Firstly I wanted to have something on the beach by the sea, although as it happens the central panel isn't very much by the sea, but in the background I used the same colour as the sky in the outer panels. I think that, when images drop in to me, although the paintings don't end up in the way the images drop in, the images themselves are suggestive of the way I can hope that chance and accident will work for me. I always think of myself not so much as a painter but as a medium for accident and chance.

DS  Why do you say that?

FB  Because I think perhaps I am unique in that way; and perhaps it's a vanity to say such a thing. But I don't think I'm gifted. I just think I'm receptive.

DS  To some energy in the ether, so to speak?

FB  I think I'm energetic in myself and I think I'm very receptive to energy. By all this I hope you won't get the idea that I think I'm inspired – I just think that I receive.

DS  Do you feel that you might have worked in another medium – that you might have been a poet, that you might have been a film-maker?

FB  No, no. I think I even might make a film; I might make a film of all the images which have crowded into my brain, which I remember and haven't used. After all, most of my paintings are to do with images. I never look at a painting, hardly. If I go to the National Gallery and I look at one of the great paintings that excite me there, it's not so much the painting that excites me as that the painting unlocks all kinds of valves of sensation within me which return me to life more violently. I might make a film, but that would be even more complicated because I wouldn't be able ever to find the image which I can make with my painting. I don't know if in another medium things would come to me as easily as they are thrown down to me in my painting.

DS  That does seem to mean that painting is your medium.

FB  I certainly couldn't have been a poet.

DS  What makes you think that?

FB  Well, because, much as I love poetry, much as it has influenced me, I don't feel, myself, that that is the way my imagination works. I don't think I could have been anything else. One doesn't know. After all, I'm an old man now. Perhaps if I was very young I would be a film-maker: it's a most marvellous medium. But I don't know. I feel I'm essentially .... Everything that I do goes into painting.

DS  At the same time, you don't feel that you're particularly gifted as a painter.

FB  No. I think that I have this peculiar kind of sensibility as a painter, where things are handed to me and I just use them. □ □ □

**6**

DS   You've been painting a lot of self-portraits. Though you said you weren't going to do any more, in fact you've done more than ever.

FB   Exactly. It's just expediency: there wasn't anyone else around to paint.

DS   It's not that you've become more involved in the problem of doing self-portraits?

FB   No.

DS   In doing them do you use photographs? Do you look in the mirror?

109 *Three Studies for a Self-Portrait* 1976

110 (Opposite) Left-hand panel of *109*

FB   I look at myself in the mirror and I look at photographs of myself as well.

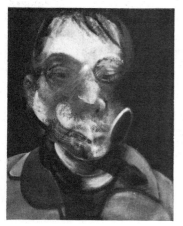 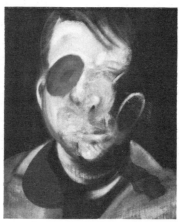 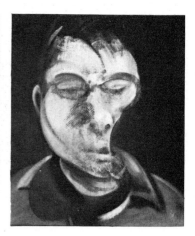

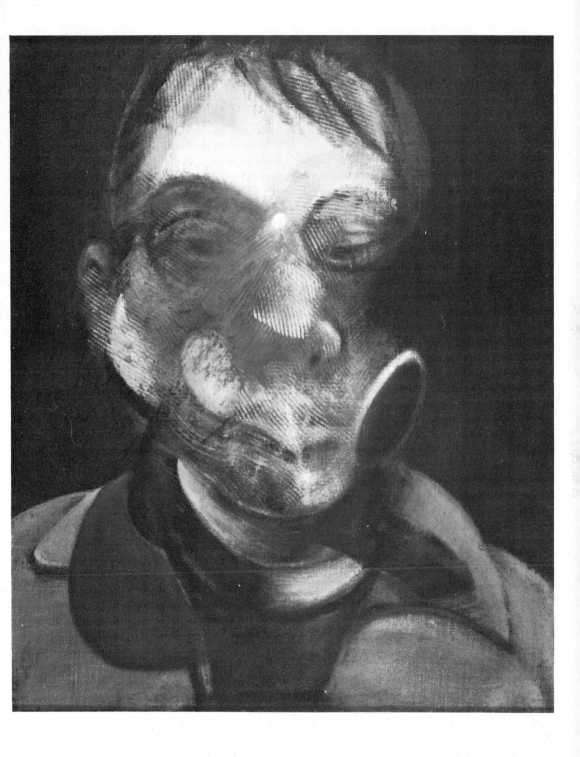

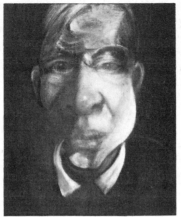
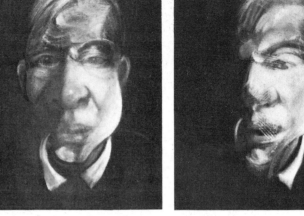

111 *Three Studies for Self-Portrait*
1979

DS  If you're using photographs, you could use photographs of someone else.

FB  I could. That's true.

DS  You haven't done any heads of George lately?

FB  No. It's always more difficult – or seems more difficult to me – to do heads of people who are dead.

DS  Yes.

FB  I don't know that it does make much difference really whether one paints things of people who are dead or alive. I mean, if you don't need the model before you. . . . But the thing is, painting myself is really expediency because, well, I was *there*, and I just hadn't got anybody else at that time to paint. As you say, I could paint from photographs. But sometimes one needs to see the person, also, while one's painting.

DS  And you've done so, of course. I suddenly realize that, when you were doing portraits from photographs of Isabel or Lucian or Henrietta, they were around a great deal, weren't they?

FB  Yes, they were. But I suppose I see really fewer and fewer people. I think one tends to do that with age.

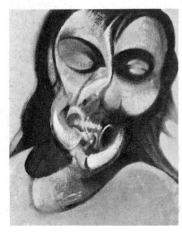

112 *Study of Henrietta Moraes*
1969

113 (Opposite) Right-hand panel of *111*

DS  So, although you weren't actually painting from them, you might have seen them the night before, and that would have made the memory of them vivid again. It all suggests that, really, the photographs are much less important than your memory of how people are.

144

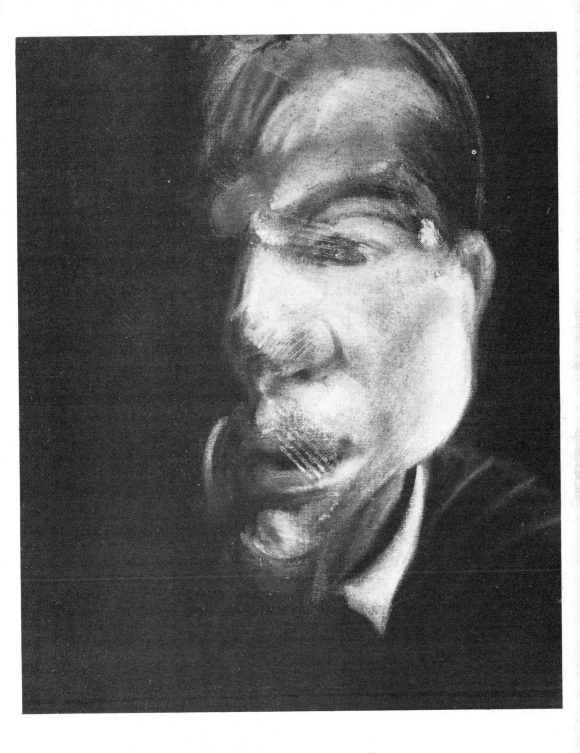

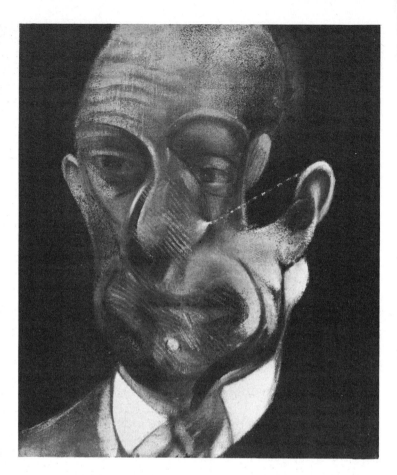

114 *Portrait of Michel Leiris* 1978

115 (Opposite) *Portrait of Michel Leiris* 1976

FB  Well, yes. I suppose yes and no. Because I'm always hoping to deform people into appearance; I can't paint them literally. For instance, I think that, of those two paintings of Michel Leiris, the one I did which is less literally like him is in fact more poignantly like him. What is curious about that particular one of Michel is that it does look more like him and yet, if you think about Michel's head, it's rather globular, in fact, and this is long and narrow. So that one doesn't know what makes one thing seem more real than another. I really wanted these portraits of Michel to look like him: there's no point in doing a portrait of somebody if you're not going to make it look like him. But, being rather long and thin, that head in fact has nothing to do with what Michel's head is really like, and yet it looks more like him. At least *I think* it looks more like him. But that is always one of the things in painting that is really impossible to explain. And I would like to make my pictures more and more artificial, more and

**146**

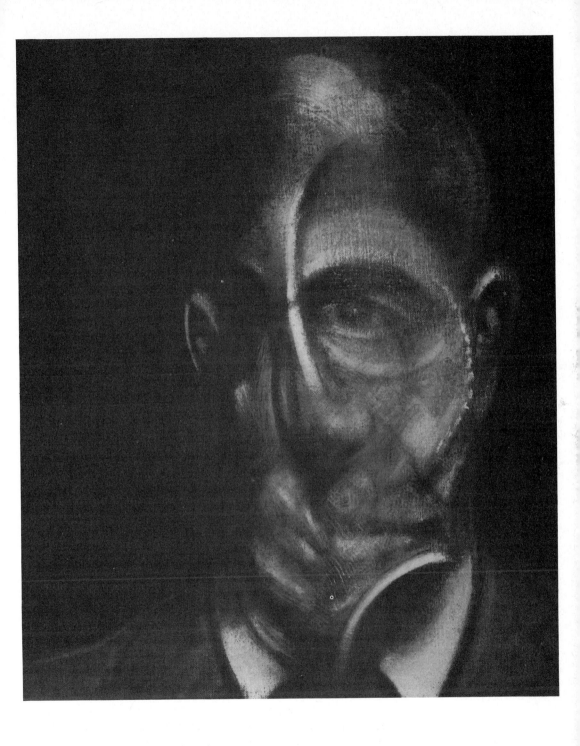

more what is called distorted – well, certainly more and more artificial. For instance, in a painting I'm trying to do of a beach and a wave breaking on it, I feel that the only possibility of doing it will be to put the beach and the wave on a kind of structure which will show them so that you take them out of their position, as it were, and re-make the wave and a piece of the beach in a very artificial structure. In this painting, I have been trying to make the structure and then hope chance will throw down the beach and the wave for me. But I just hope that this painting, no matter how artificial it is, will be like a wave breaking on a seashore.

DS  You want to make it like?

FB  I want to make it like but I don't know how to make it like.

DS  But you're sure that you can only make it like in a very oblique way?

FB  Yes. That I'm sure of. Otherwise, I'd just do one more picture of a sea and a seashore.

DS  What will make it something that isn't just one more picture?

FB  Only if I can take it far enough away from being another picture, if I can elevate, as it were, the shore and the wave – almost cut it out as a fragment and elevate it within the whole picture so that it looks so artificial and yet so much more real than if it were a painting of the sea breaking on the shore.

DS  You're wanting it to look both real and artificial?

FB  Yes.

DS  You're looking for a certain unexpectedness? You're wanting to surprise yourself too?

FB  Naturally. What else would you go on painting for?

DS  And what's the surprise? That the more artificial the thing gets, the more like it gets.

FB  Yes. The more artificial you can make it, the greater chance you've got of its looking real.

DS  Now, it's clear that in any art there's a mixture of intention and what takes the artist by surprise.

FB   Yes. Without the intention, he's not going to start at all.

DS   What you seem to say is that in your own case surprise takes over from intention quite early on.

FB   You see, one has an intention, but what really happens comes about in working – that's the reason it's so hard to talk about it – it actually does come about in the working. And the way it works is really by the things that happen. In working you are really following this kind of cloud of sensation in yourself, but you don't know what it really is. And it's called instinct. And one's instinct, whether right or wrong, fixes on certain things that have happened in that activity of applying the paint to the canvas. I think an awful lot of creation is made out of, also, the self-criticism of an artist, and very often I think probably what makes one artist seem better than another is that his critical sense is more acute. It may not be that he is more gifted in any way but just that he has a better critical sense.

DS   And in the application of his critical sense, he has no defined criteria; it's a purely instinctive kind of criticism. Is that what you mean?

FB   I do mean that; yes. And he will never know whether he was right or not to leave it, because, after all, it takes too long really to know whether things are any good or not.

DS   This painting of a wave: did the idea come to you in the way you've talked about ideas you've had before – like dropping into your mind like slides?

FB   No, I just happened to see it. I just happened to see the sea break when I was down in the South of France some months ago.

DS   Does that happen often, that some particular moment or scene fixes itself in your mind?

FB   I've done so little in landscape or seascape that it hasn't happened a great deal. And it happens less, you see, with people.

DS   It happens less with people?

FB   Yes, because they are people I know. Do you see what I mean? For instance, I just happened to see this wave breaking in this way.

DS  Do you not sometimes, with someone you know, in your room, see a certain gesture, a certain turn of the head, of the body, that stays in your mind as something you want to recapture in a painting?

FB  No, not in the same way. With the body, it's generally just that I want to do the body in a certain position.

DS  What makes you do a figure turning a key in a door with his foot?

FB  I think that came – I don't know why I made it turn with the foot – it very much came from that poem of Eliot's: 'I have heard the key/Turn in the door once and turn once only. . . .' You know. It comes from *The Waste Land*. I don't know why I should have made it turn with the foot. But it did come from that poem. I don't know why I made it turn with the foot.

DS  It's a marvellous example of the interplay of intention and result. The intention, the Eliot image, that's your private thing.

FB  Absolutely.

DS  It's not visible in the work.

FB  Not at all.

DS  While the thing that's most evident in the work, the thing the picture seems to be about, was unplanned.

FB  Yes. I suppose those things perhaps come through from Surrealism too, to some extent. It's that one thinks it's going to be more immediate somehow, if the key is being turned by the foot than if it is turned, as it usually is, by the hand.

DS  Yes, it does relate to Surrealism, doesn't it? I mean, Magritte was always writing about the mystery of banal reality and of his wanting to use painting to evoke that mystery. But he painted a fruit or a loaf floating in mid-air; he displaced the thing to make a mystery that was more immediate, although, as he said, a fruit or a loaf on a table is full of mystery.

FB  Yes, that's very much the same thing as turning the key with the foot.

DS  I never guessed there was any connection between this painting and Eliot, though I know well that you've always

116 (Opposite) *Painting 1978*

150

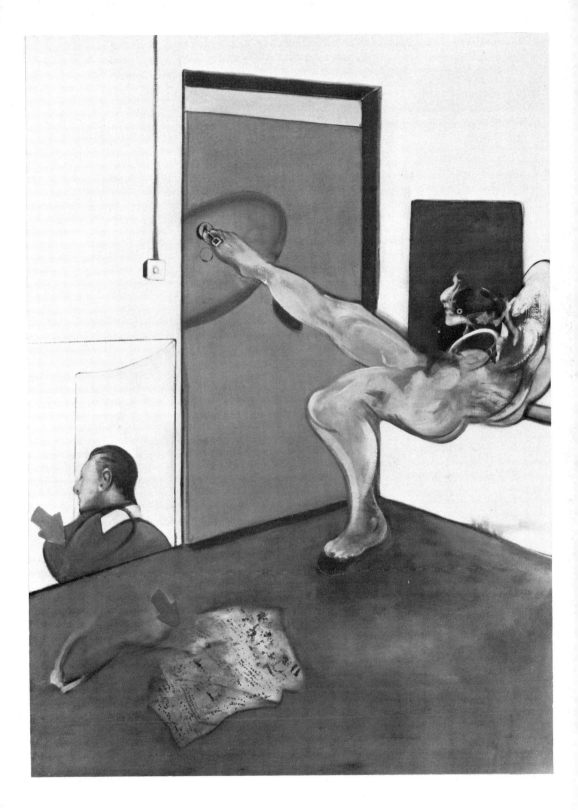

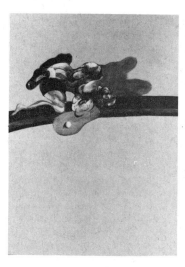
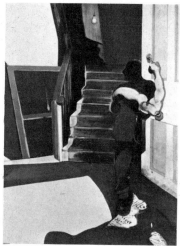
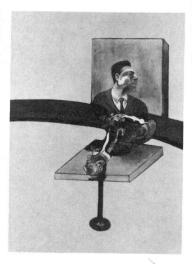

117 *Triptych 1971*

118 (Opposite) Centre panel of *117*

been haunted by *The Waste Land*. Are there other lines of his that have actually inspired particular paintings? Apart from the *Sweeney Agonistes* triptych, of course.

FB I always feel I've been influenced by Eliot. *The Waste Land* especially and the poems before it have always affected me very much. And I often read the *Four Quartets*, and I think perhaps they're even greater poetry than *The Waste Land*, though they don't move me in the same way. But I've hardly ever done things directly inspired by particular lines or poems. I admire them and they excite me and they goad me to try and work much more. That is the way they influence me. It's very difficult to use any poetry for one's painting: it's the whole atmosphere of it that affects one. I've also been very affected by a great number of Yeats's poems. Perhaps one thing I admire so much about Yeats is the way he made himself – perhaps he was always a remarkable poet, but he seems to me to have really worked on himself in a quite extraordinary way. But we're talking about modern poets, and you would find the whole of Eliot and Yeats and everything and practically every other poet in Shakespeare, who just enlivens life, no matter how futile you think it is, in a way that nobody else has ever been able to do. He just opens it out in such an extraordinary way. He enlivens it both by his profound despair and pessimism and also by, you may say, his humour. And his absolutely, really, in a way, diabolical cynicism. I mean, what can be more cynical than Macbeth at the end, in 'To-morrow, and to-morrow, and to-morrow'?

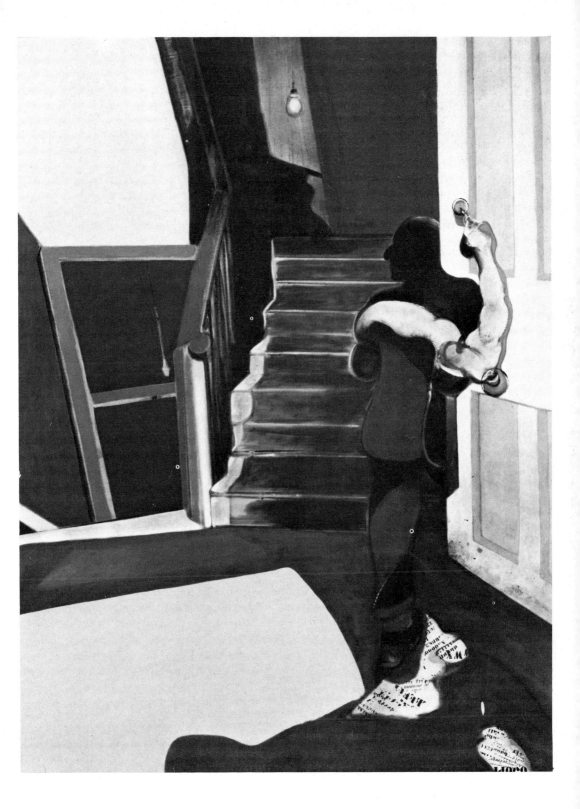

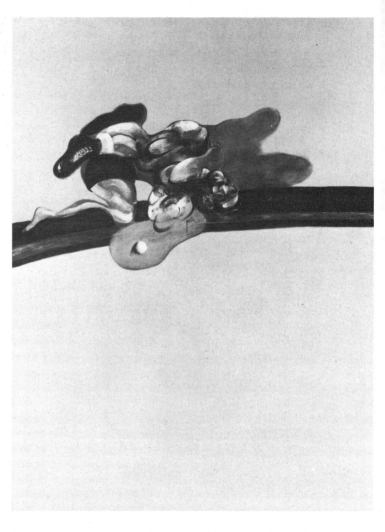

119 Left-hand panel of *117*

Do you want me to get it for you? Because I was just reading it today, and I thought, well, once again it really is about the most extraordinary summing-up. □ □ □

120 (Opposite) *Figure in movement* 1976

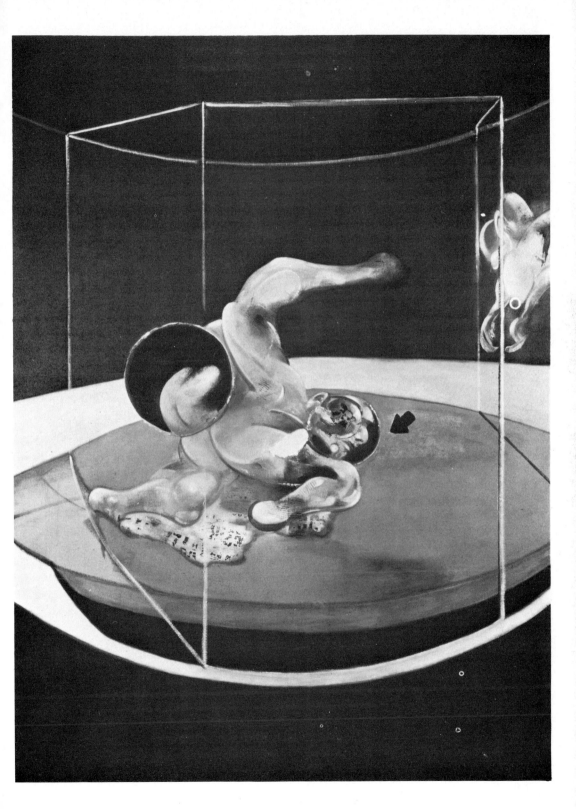

## 7

DS   When we were trying to fix a date to do this and we'd agreed on a day and a time, I said that I'd ring you that morning to see if you felt in the mood and you said you never felt in the mood, any more than you felt in the mood to paint before you actually started.

FB   Well, it is very much like that. As you work, the mood grows on you. There *are* certain images which suddenly get hold of me and I really want to do them. But it's true to say that the excitement and the possibilities are in the working and obviously can only come in working.

121 *Triptych – Studies of the Human Body 1979*

122 (Opposite) Centre panel of *121*

DS   So you start painting every day, more or less? Not only on days when you feel a bit inspired to start?

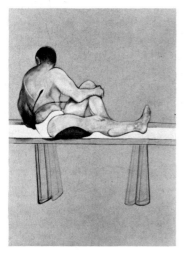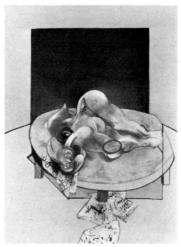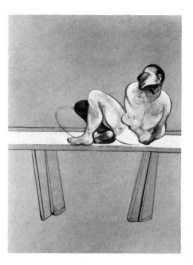

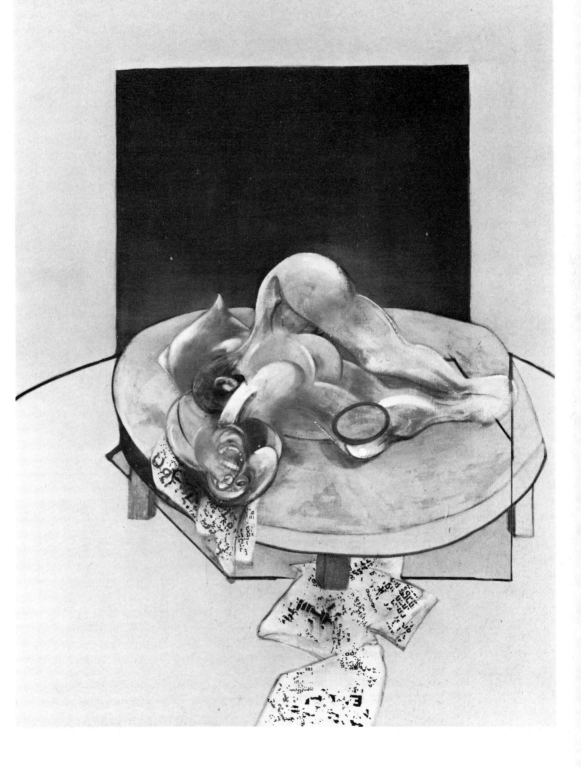

FB No. I don't really know what people mean by inspiration. Certainly, there are things called good runs, when you start and the thing seems to work for you and as you go along you seem to be able to be carried along by it. I don't know if that's what they mean by inspiration. Or is it a kind of pressure within to start doing something? I suppose there are different interpretations.

DS Even if you get up feeling out of sorts and hung over, you'll still go on with the picture that you're doing?

FB Yes, generally.

DS And if you like the way it was at the end of yesterday and you feel that you might be in a disastrous state for working, will you still go on with the picture?

FB Well, I often wish that I had a camera and just took the thing as it went along, because, certainly, very often in working one loses the best moments of a painting in trying to take it further. And, if one had a record of what it was, one might be able to find it again. So it would almost be nice to have a running camera going all the time that one was working.

DS Are there days when, having started, you give up after an hour?

FB Yes. Yes. I just get bored. I know nothing is going to come.

DS And are there days when you paint eight or nine hours?

FB Yes, there are. That's generally when you are always on the edge of possibility and it's always escaping you. But then that's how it always is generally. But nevertheless it seems on those days – you seem to be nearer and it seems to evade you more resolutely.

DS Do you have long periods now of not working?

FB Not very long, no.

DS In the past you did tend to.

FB In the past I did, but I go on working now. I've got so many things I want to do, and there seems to be such a short time left to do it all in.

DS In the past there were times when you were working

hard for three or four months and then sort of needed a break of a few weeks.

FB   Oh, I don't need a break; no one needs a break, really. That's just an idea. I mean, after all, I hate holidays.

DS   But you used to take breaks before?

FB   I did. But those were the times when I was emotionally involved with people. Now I'm not emotionally involved with people.

DS   Did you find that, when you were very involved in painting, it tended to get in the way of your emotional life?

FB   It was the opposite way round. My emotional life tended to get in the way of my painting.

DS   I think there are some painters who manage to keep everything going together.

FB   Yes, well, some people are lucky.

DS   But not you?

FB   . Not very. □ □ □


DS   You said long ago that if anything ever works in your case it does so from that moment when consciously you don't know what you're doing. Do you think it's possible to encourage that state while working by making a conscious effort to relax, in the hope that through that relaxation one would be more open?

FB   Well, I've never been a person who *can* relax, in any case. I can hardly sit down for long. I've never been able to sit in a comfortable chair. And if I'm here, even alone, I hardly ever sit down, I just walk about or . . . . I do sit for a bit if I'm reading, perhaps, but in the ordinary way I'm completely unrelaxed. It's one of the reasons I've suffered all my life from high blood-pressure. People say: relax! What *do* they mean? I never understand this thing where people relax their muscles and they relax everything – I don't know how to do it. So it's no use my talking about relaxation because it is something I have never experienced. The only time . . . . I remember when I was very young and had very, very bad asthma and I used to be given injections of morphia; it was certainly marvellous then, the relaxation that the morphia

**159**

gave one. They never gave one enough because they always thought one would become addicted. But it's certainly a thing I always look back on.

DS   Doesn't drink make you relax?

FB   It makes me very talkative, but whether it relaxes me or not I don't know. It makes me garrulous.

DS   I must say that in social situations, I've seldom seen you unrelaxed. Or *looking* unrelaxed. It's perhaps that you're a very good actor.

FB   It's my social upbringing. It's also having lived a long time and seen all types of people.

DS   I don't understand how you can have this receptiveness to chance if you're as tense as you say you are.

FB   You see, you don't know how the hopelessness in one's working will make one just take paint and just do almost anything to get out of the formula of making a kind of illustrative image – I mean, I just wipe it all over with a rag or use a brush or rub it with something or anything or throw turpentine and paint and everything else onto the thing to try to break the willed articulation of the image, so that the image will grow, as it were, spontaneously and within its own structure, and not my structure. Afterwards, your sense of what you want comes into play, so that you begin to work on the hazard that has been left to you on the canvas. And out of all that, possibly, a more organic image arises than if it was a willed image.

DS   You're saying that at the crucial times you may be working quite frantically?

FB   Yes.

DS   So, if there is relaxation, it'll be likely to come after the point has arrived where the critical sense comes into play?

FB   Certainly one is more relaxed when the image that one has within one's sensations – you see, there is a kind of sensational image within the very, you could say, structure of your being, which is not to do with a mental image – when that image, through accident, begins to form. Then I think your critical side comes into play and you begin to construct on this basis which seems to have been organically, by

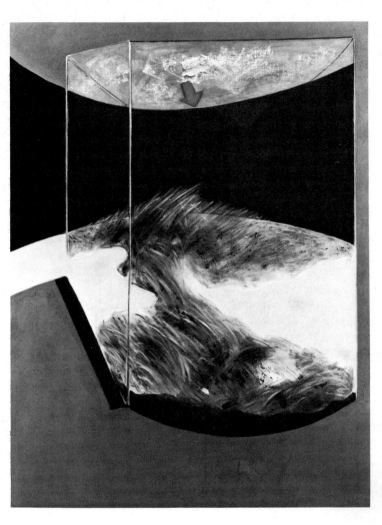

123 *Landscape* 1978

chance, given to you. It probably sounds nonsense, as it's a thing which you can't be clear about, since you don't know what it is, beyond knowing that your sensibility attaches itself to one image rather than another because you feel that that image is more organic than another. For instance, I can think of that picture I've done of some grass, a landscape that I wanted to put into a frame. I wanted it to be a landscape and look unlike a landscape. And so I whittled it down and down until in the end there was just a little stretch of grass left which I enclosed in the box. And that really came about by trying to cut away, out of despair, the look of what is called a landscape. I wanted it to be a landscape that didn't look like a landscape. I don't know if it at all succeeded.

DS  Well, for me this landscape, this grass, is filled with an

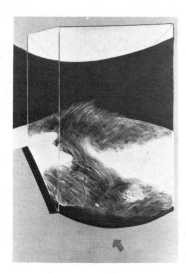

124 First state of *123*

125 (Opposite) *Jet of Water* 1979

extraordinary animal energy. Whether that's something you would want it to have I don't know.

FB  I want it to have it. I don't know whether it does have it.

DS  Was it part of your aim that it should have it?

FB  No.

DS  If it's there, it came because you were trying to eliminate something?

FB  Yes.

DS  Another thing. Does the painting just come out of a sort of general memory of grass? Or does it derive from something particular you've seen?

FB  Yes, it does. It was a marvellous photograph I had of grass, and the photograph had got torn up and it formed to some extent the shape that the grass has. It kept on being trampled on so much in all the chaos of where I work, and, when I pulled it out, it had practically all fallen away, but there was just this sort of fragment of grass left.

DS  Did the painting come more-or-less quickly or more-or-less slowly?

FB  Well, after letting it go, I had it brought back to the studio and did some more to it. The first time, the background colour was a kind of fawn – it was the colour of canvas – but I felt I wanted it to be much more artificial. So – I don't know whether correctly or not – I added that whole very intense surround of cobalt blue, which I felt made it look more completely artificial and unreal. I wanted that really strong blue to take all naturalism out of it.

DS  There's a painting which I take to be the counterpart, as a seascape, of the one of grass as a landscape. You say you wanted a landscape that didn't look like a landscape, and in the other you seem to have wanted a seascape that didn't look like a seascape. It's the painting, of course, that was meant to be of a wave breaking on the shore but ended up as a jet of water. Could you tell me how that transformation happened?

FB  Well, I collected an enormous amount of paint, and I didn't really mix them, I put them all into a pot, and I had painted the background in, and I just threw the paint onto the canvas, as you can see; I threw on what I hoped to be a wave,

**162**

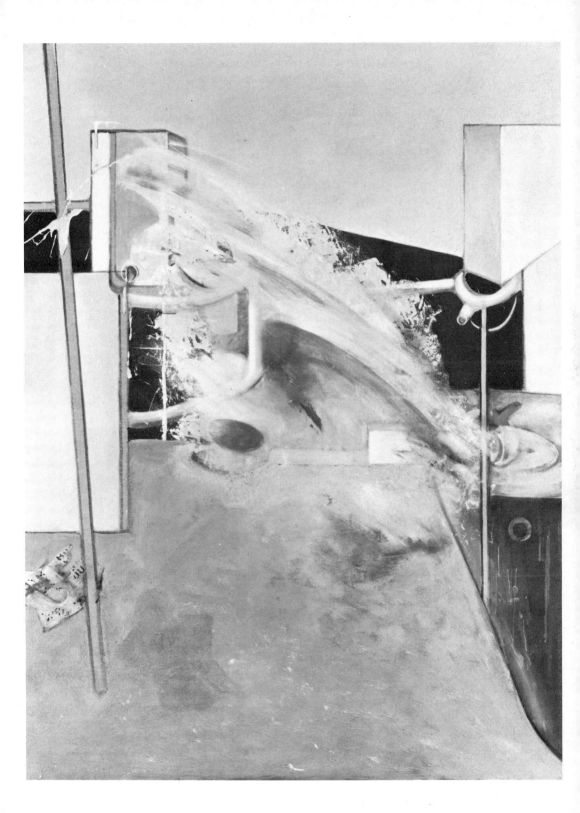

and it didn't make a wave. But there were lots of things about it that I liked, and it wasn't going to be a wave; it looked more like a jet of water, so I turned it into a jet of water.

DS  When you say that you'd painted the background in before throwing on paint, does what you call the background include the machinery?

FB  Yes. I'd manufactured that kind of industrial background to it, and I thought I would make the wave break – instead of breaking against the shore – against this industrial structure. But it nevertheless didn't; it turned more into a jet of water than into a wave, so I had to concentrate on trying to make it a jet of water against this industrial structure, which of course is more normal than it would have been: it would have been more exciting if it had been a wave against an industrial background. Perhaps I should have known that, once one had made that structure, if one put in water, it would become a jet of water rather than a wave. It was probably just my stupidity. Perhaps one day I shall be able to paint a wave breaking on the shore.

DS  But do you think that the *Jet of Water* itself is going to give rise to other images?

FB  I think one always has more images than one can deal with, so that's not a problem – at any rate, it's not a problem for me. I have far more images than I shall ever be able to do – images that drop in from time to time to me that I shall never be able to use.

DS  I don't think many painters now could say that. I think that most of them have this terrific problem – it seems to me to show very much in their painting – that they don't really know what to paint.

FB  Are you now talking about abstract painters?

DS  Yes, but also about figurative painters.

FB  But there is the image. The problem is how you're going to make the figuration. How are you going to make this thing look real, how are you going to make it real to the way you feel about the thing or real to the instinct?

DS  The fact that you can say that the problem for a figurative painter is only how to make it real shows just how far you take it for granted that a painter knows what image he wants to try and make.

126 (Opposite) Right-hand panel of *127*

164

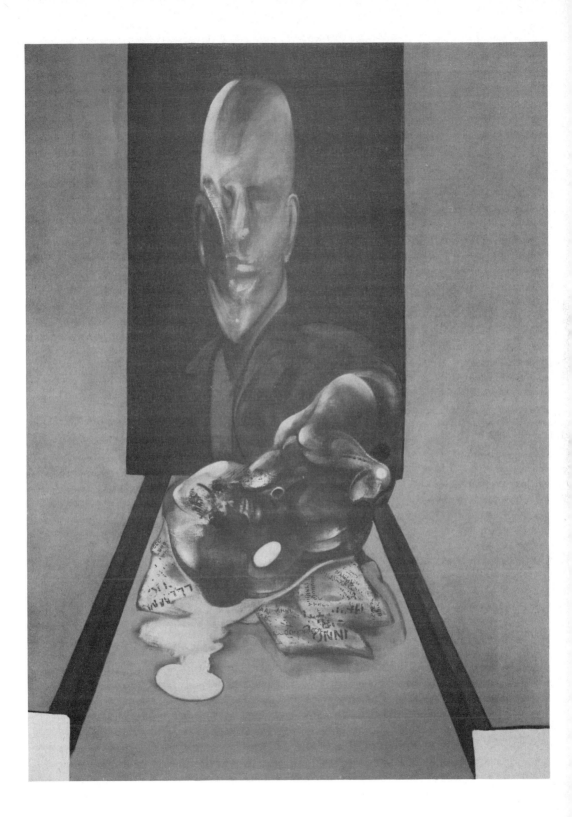

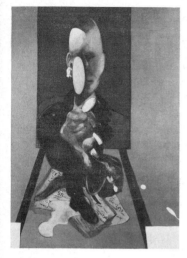 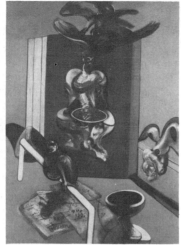 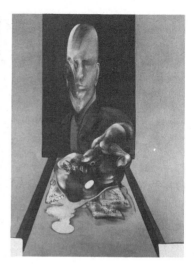

127 *Triptych 1976*

128 (Opposite) Centre panel of
*127*

FB  I suppose it's that I'm not short of images at all; I have thousands of them. That's not a problem. I don't see why it ever should be a problem for a painter – for any real painter. By saying that, I don't think I'm a real painter either, but I happen to be very, very full of images.

DS  Well, I think that a lot of the problem of the artist today, and the sort of impotence one feels in art today, is that people actually don't know what to paint.

FB  I think that's possible. Well, certainly, one's never felt it either with the Impressionists or with Cézanne that there was ever for a moment a question of their not knowing what to do. And I've certainly never felt it with Picasso, though occasionally I've felt it with Matisse: much of Picasso I don't like, but nevertheless I've never felt for one second that he was ever short of images. And I suppose I'm lucky in that images just drop in as if they were handed down to me. Really, I think of myself as a maker of images. The image matters more than the beauty of the paint.

DS  And the mystery of the paint?

FB  If you can make the image with the mystery of the paint, so much the better.

DS  Well, I think that the grass and the jet are very much among the paintings of yours in which that happens. Incidentally, do *you* see an erotic content in the jet? I know it couldn't have been consciously intended; that's obvious from the way the thing was done.

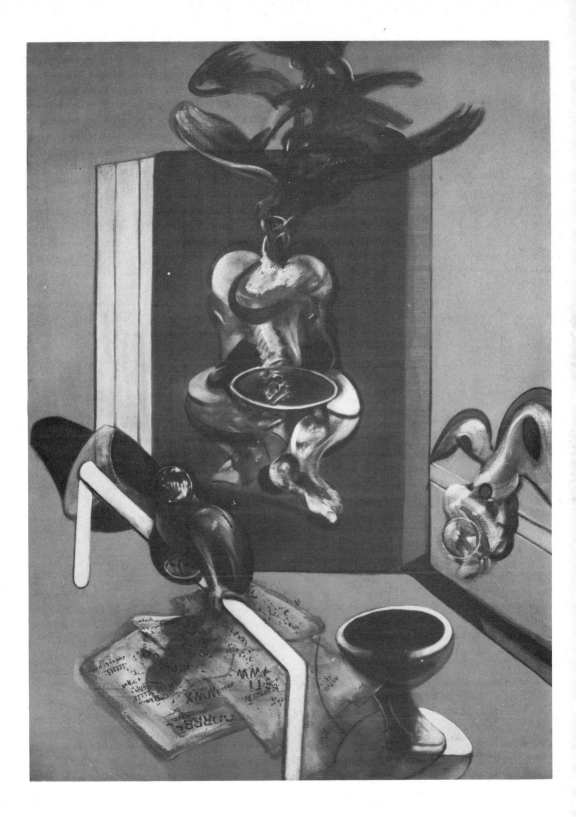

FB   For me it's just a jet of water.

DS   Perhaps I see it as something else as well because for me the picture, like the one of grass, has a sort of animal energy – not an elemental, macrocosmic energy but an energy that has an animal, even a human, scale.

FB   What I would like those things to be would be an essence, you might say, of landscape and an essence of water. That's what I would like them to be.

DS   There's another recent painting of yours, of a figure, which looks to me as if it might be taking the same sort of direction – the one called *Figure in movement*. And when you talk about essence, and about whittling down, I wonder whether there was something of the same intention in this painting.

FB   Yes, there was. It comes very much into that category. It was an attempt to make a figure in movement as concentrated as I could do it. Perhaps that is why painting is an old man's occupation, and perhaps, so long as one can work, one may be able to get nearer to a kind of essence of these things. □ □ □

129 (Opposite) *Figure in movement* 1978

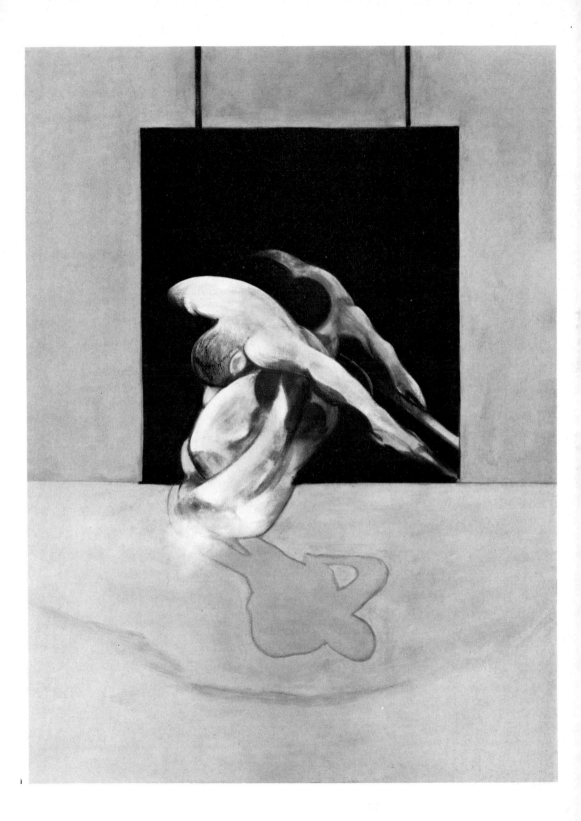

8

DS   Michel Leiris speaks of ways in which your work is a form of realism. What do you think yourself that 'realism' means today?

FB   I think that our sense of realism has been changed to some extent since Surrealism – well, really, since Freud – because we've been made more conscious of how realism can draw on the unconscious. And I think a very good example is certain work done by Picasso in the years around 1930, such as the small paintings he did at Dinard – I think it was in 1928 – of figures on the beach. As Picasso, I believe, absorbed everything, he absorbed Surrealism, and those images are profoundly unillustrative but profoundly real about figures. For instance, a curious curved image unlocking the door of a bathing cabin is far more real than if it was an illustration of a figure unlocking the door of a bathing cabin.

DS   I notice that you've been saying 'more real' rather than 'more realist' or 'more realistic'.

FB   Well, 'real' is surely only a way of talking about realism, isn't it?

DS   It might not be. It might be a way of saying that the forms had more inherent reality for you – in other words, more weight, more presence.

FB   No, when I say it's 'more real', I mean that that gesture of somebody turning the key in a door was more real done that way than if it had been more illustrational.

130 (Opposite) Picasso *Bather and Cabin* 1928

DS   More realistic, you mean, done that way?

**170**

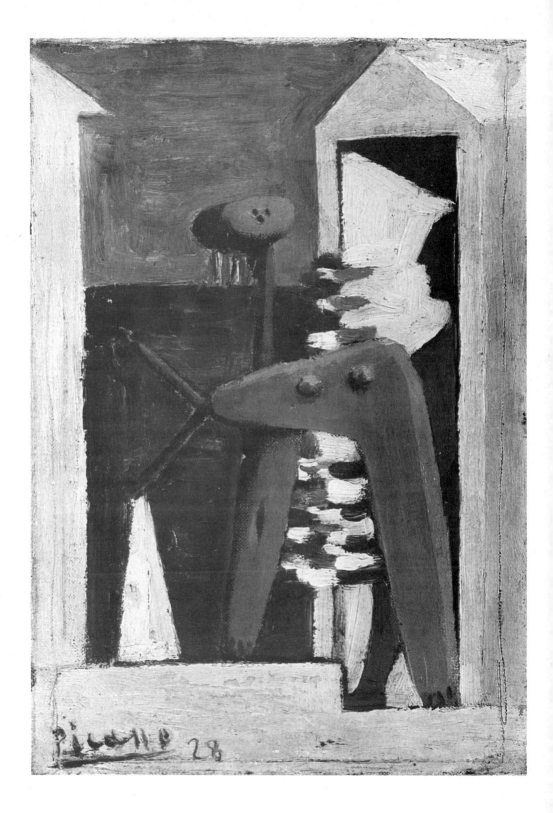

FB  Well, you can call it if you like 'realistic'. No. I don't see why 'real' doesn't stand for realistic. When I say 'more real' I mean more factual.

DS  Now, does the reality which that Picasso image has for you owe something to the contrast between the quite literal rendering of the key and the keyhole and the invented character of the figure? I mean, does this contrast throw into relief the force of the gesture?

FB  I think so. I think that it brings in not only the external reality but it brings in the unconscious reality of turning the key in the lock, which has subjective implications, and these are what gives a poignancy to the key being inserted into the lock. I believe that realism has to be re-invented. It has to be continuously re-invented. In one of his letters Van Gogh speaks of the need to make changes in reality, which become lies that are truer than the literal truth. This is the only possible way the painter can bring back the intensity of the reality which he is trying to capture. I believe that reality in art is something profoundly artificial and that it has to be re-created. Otherwise it will be just an illustration of something – which will be very second-hand.

DS  Yes. Now, when you re-create it and make out of it a form or an image which has a particular force of presence, is the factor in this form that moves us not the vitality it seems to embody and the sort of grandeur or whatever it may be that we sense in a form? Is our response to it not a response to its inherent qualities, which obviously connect with our experience – very much so – but not in a way that amounts to our making a comparison of it with something else? If you say that a thing is like something in reality, you have to compare it with reality to confirm that. But isn't it the case, when we look at a great work of art and are moved by it, that we don't make such comparisons, that the work has a kind of power of its own which speaks to us?

FB  Yes, certainly, of course it has. It has its own power. Because it has re-invented its own realism. And Van Gogh is one of my great heroes because I think that he was able to be almost literal and yet by the way he put on the paint give you a marvellous vision of the reality of things. I saw it very clearly when I was once in Provence and going through that part of the Crau where he did some of his landscapes, and one just saw in this absolutely barren country that by the way he put on the paint he was able to give it such an amazing living

131 (Opposite) *Figure Writing Reflected in a Mirror* 1976

172

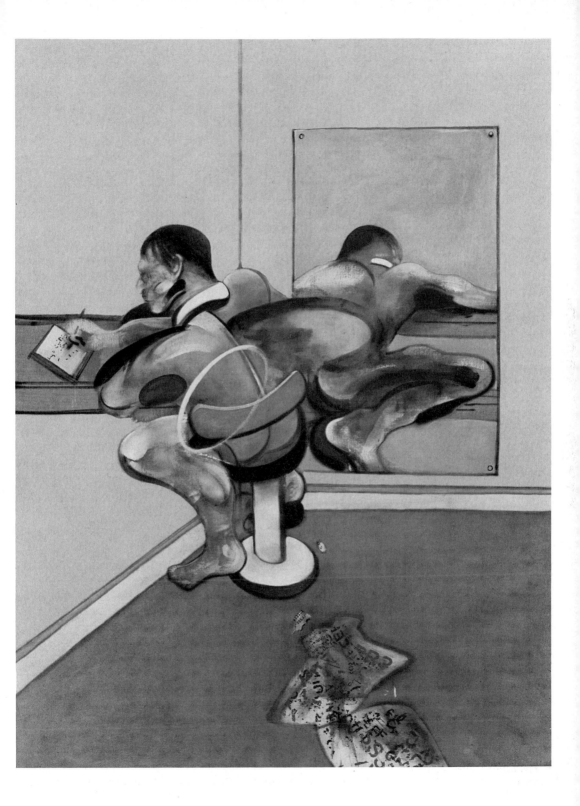

quality, give that reality the Crau has of just plain, bare land. The living quality is what you have to get. In painting a portrait the problem is to find a technique by which you can give over all the pulsations of a person. It's why portrait painting is so fascinating and so difficult. Most people go to the most academic painters when they want to have their portraits made because for some reason they prefer a sort of colour photograph of themselves instead of thinking of having themselves really trapped and caught. The sitter is someone of flesh and blood and what has to be caught is their emanation. I'm not talking in a spiritual way or anything like that – that is the last thing I believe in. But there are always emanations from people whoever they are, though some people's are stronger than others'.

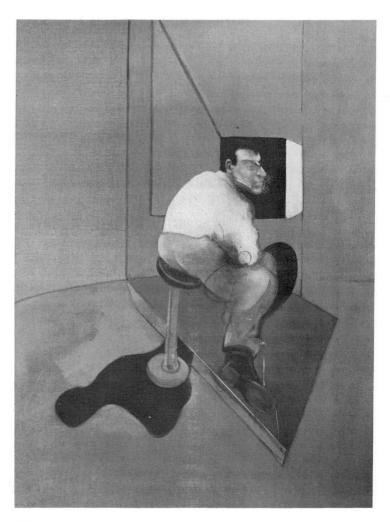

132 *Study for a Portrait of John Edwards* 1986

DS  If you don't like the word emanation, could you talk about the kind of energy given off by someone?

FB  Energy is better. There is the appearance and there is the energy within the appearance. And that is an extremely difficult thing to trap. Of course, a person's appearance is closely linked with their energy. So that, when you are in the street and in the distance you see somebody you know, you can tell who they are just by the way they walk and by the way they move. But I don't know whether it would be possible to do a portrait of somebody just by making a gesture of them. So far it seems that if you are doing a portrait you have to record the face. But with their face you have to try and trap the energy that emanates from them.

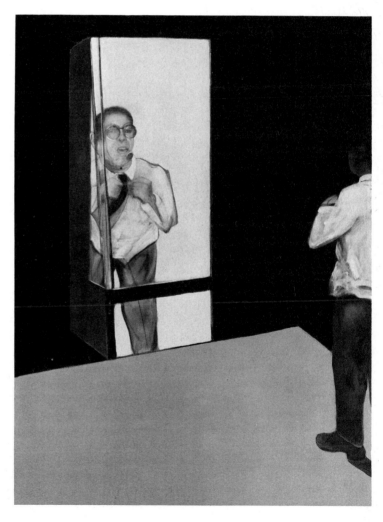

133 *Study for Portrait of Gilbert de Botton* 1986

DS So what explains the forms on your canvas is above all the attempt to capture the energy and the appearance together?

FB Yes, but with all the mechanical means of rendering appearance, it means that a painter, if he is going to attempt to record life, has to do it in a much more intense and curtailed way. It has to have the intensity of . . . you can call it sophisticated simplicity. And I don't mean the kind of simplicity Cycladic sculpture has, which simplifies into banality, but the kind Egyptian sculpture has, which simplifies into reality. You have to abbreviate into intensity.

DS But you don't just abbreviate; you also impose a certain rhythm – a distortion, some might say. You twist what you see in a certain way that is characteristic of you and it might be thought that the particular way in which you do twist things is significant of a certain attitude to life.

FB Well, I feel that that is a misreading of it. What I do with the forms is done for aesthetic reasons, is done because I think that it gives across the image in a more acute and accurate way.

DS But why does one have to distort as freely as modern artists like yourself do, rather than simply achieve that kind of abbreviation which somebody like Degas achieved?

FB Yes, but photography hadn't been developed as far in Degas's time as it has now. Another thing is, when you talk of Degas, the very great Degas are the pastels, and don't forget that in his pastels he always striates the form with these lines which are drawn through the image and in a certain sense both intensify and diversify its reality (44). I always think that the interesting thing about Degas is the way he made lines through the body: you could say that he shuttered the body, in a way, shuttered the image and then he put an enormous amount of colour through these lines. And having shuttered the form, he created intensity by putting this colour through the flesh. As the techniques of the cinema and all forms of recording become better and better, so the painter has to be more and more inventive. He has to re-invent realism. He has to wash the realism back onto the nervous system by his invention, because there isn't such a thing in painting any longer as natural realism. But does one know why very often, or nearly always, the accidental images are the most real? Perhaps they've not been

134 (Opposite) *Study for Portrait of John Edwards* 1986

**176**

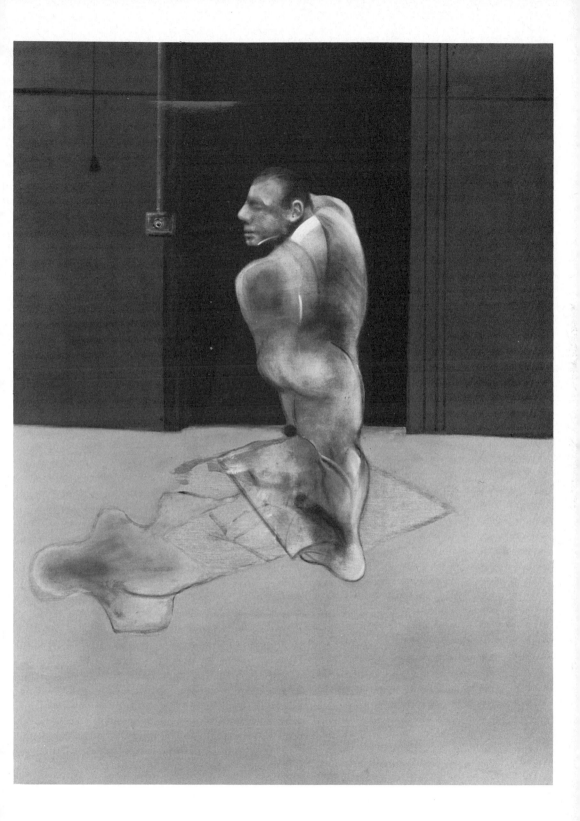

tampered with by the conscious brain and therefore come across in a much more raw and real sense than something which has been tampered with by consciousness? It is very much, of course, in that sense, like children's art – very young children's art – because one has seen how, after the age of about seven or eight, or probably even earlier than that, when they've been influenced by their environment, that all its spontaneity and vitality have gone and it just becomes very boring. But of course the trouble with children's art is that, even at its best, it is never enough.

DS   When you talk about the potency which the image has when it's come from the unconscious and hasn't been corrected by conscious thought, I suppose that the risk with the

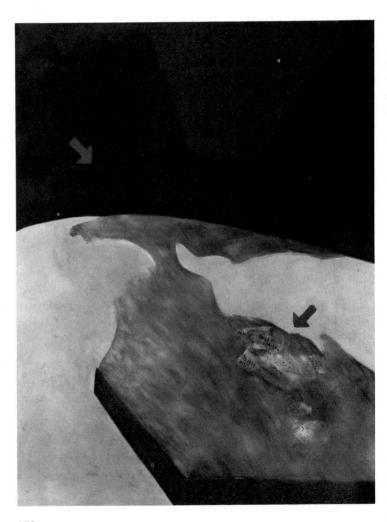

135 *A Piece of Waste Land* 1982

intervention of conscious thought would be that it would tend to push the work back towards conforming with a conventional and accepted idea of what art is. Or with what realism is. Do you think it's become impossible to create a realism the language of which is less unlike the European art of recent centuries?

FB   Well, I don't know. You may find somebody who comes along and is able to do it, but one knows very well that, with the people who have so far attempted to go back to figuration in the more accepted sense, it's been extremely weak and really meaningless.

DS   Why meaningless, do you think?

FB   Well, we're so saturated with all the arts, through all the means of reproducing them and seeing them and everything, that the saturation point has come so strongly that one just longs for new images and new ways by which reality can be created. After all, man wants invention, he doesn't want to go on and on and on just reproducing the past. I mean, it was the end of Greek art, it was the end of Egyptian art, because they went on and on and on reproducing themselves. We can't go on and on reproducing the Renaissance or nineteenth-century art or anything else. You want something new. Not an illustrative realism but a realism that comes about through a real invention of a new way to lock reality into something completely arbitrary.

DS   Completely arbitrary or completely artificial?

FB   Well, I said arbitrary, but I think artificial would have been better.

DS   Because arbitrary might be true as well, but I think a part, an essential part of the force of a thing is that while being unexpected it also looks inevitable. Would you agree with that?

FB   Yes. The person who I think got in some ways nearest to it was Marcel Duchamp in the *Large Glass*, which takes to the limit this problem of abstraction and realism.

DS   Even more than Picasso?

FB   I think so, perhaps. Especially in that it's so impervious to interpretation.

DS   I think that an example of that in your own work occurs

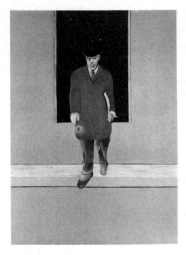 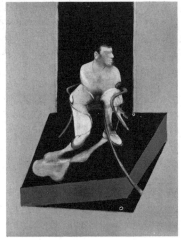 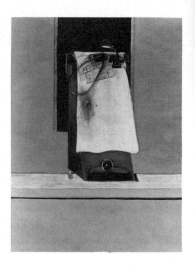

136 *Triptych* 1986–7

in those recent paintings of a male nude into which you have introduced a batsman's pads – taken, I imagine, from a book of photographs of David Gower which I've seen in your studio.

FB   Well, I have often seen cricket. And when I did this image I suddenly said, well, I don't know why, but I think it's going to strengthen it very much and make it look very much more real if it has cricket pads on it. I can't tell you why.

DS   It seems to me from all that you've been saying that in the end what matters most to you is not an immediacy in the work's reference to reality, but a tension between juxtaposed references to different realities and the tension between a reference to reality and the artificial structure by which it's made.

FB   Well, it's in the artificial structure that the reality of the subject will be caught, and the trap will close over the subject-matter and leave only the reality. One always starts work with the subject, no matter how tenuous it is, and one constructs an artificial structure by which one can trap the reality of the subject-matter that one has started from.

DS   The subject's a sort of bait?

FB   The subject is the bait.

DS   And what is that reality that remains, that residue? How does it relate to what you began with?

137 (Opposite) Centre panel of *136*

FB   It doesn't necessarily relate to it, but you will have

180

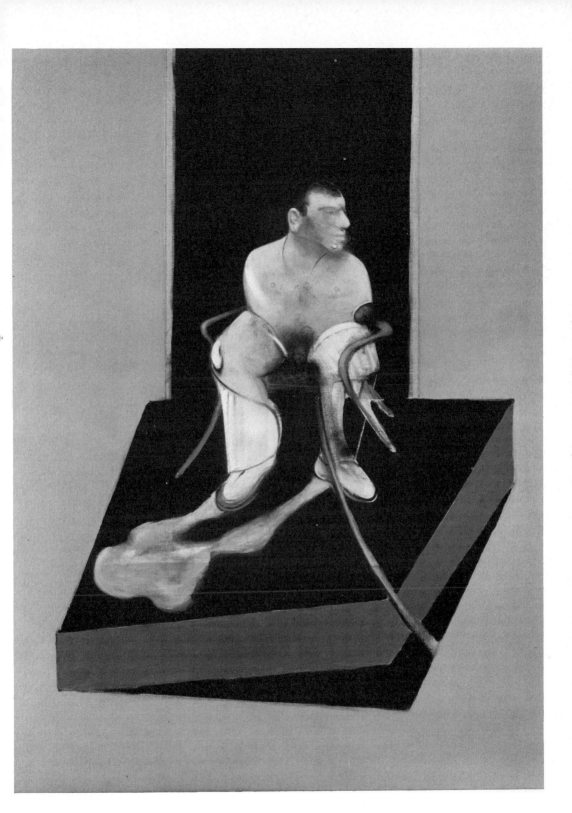

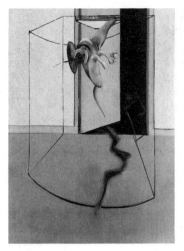 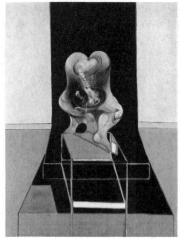 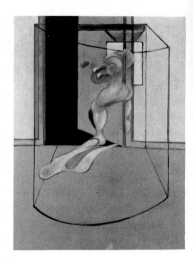

138 *Triptych – inspired by the Oresteia of Aeschylus* 1981

created a realism equivalent to the subject-matter which will be what is left in its place. You have to start from somewhere, and you start from the subject which gradually, if the thing works at all, withers away and leaves this residue which we call reality and which perhaps has something tenuously to do with what one started with but very often has very little to do with it.

DS   And speaking of realism in the way you do, where do you put Matisse's late *papiers découpés*, especially those single nudes, one or two of which you've told me you admired?

FB   I have never had the strong feeling that many people have about Matisse; I've always found him too lyrical and decorative. I think he is less so than usual in some of the late *papiers découpés*, but nevertheless for me there is very little realism in Matisse. I think it's the reason I have always been so much more interested in Picasso. Because Matisse never had the – what can one say? – the brutality of fact which Picasso had. I don't think he ever had the invention of Picasso and I think he turns fact into lyricism. He doesn't have Picasso's brutality of fact. □ □ □

139 (Opposite) Centre panel of *138*

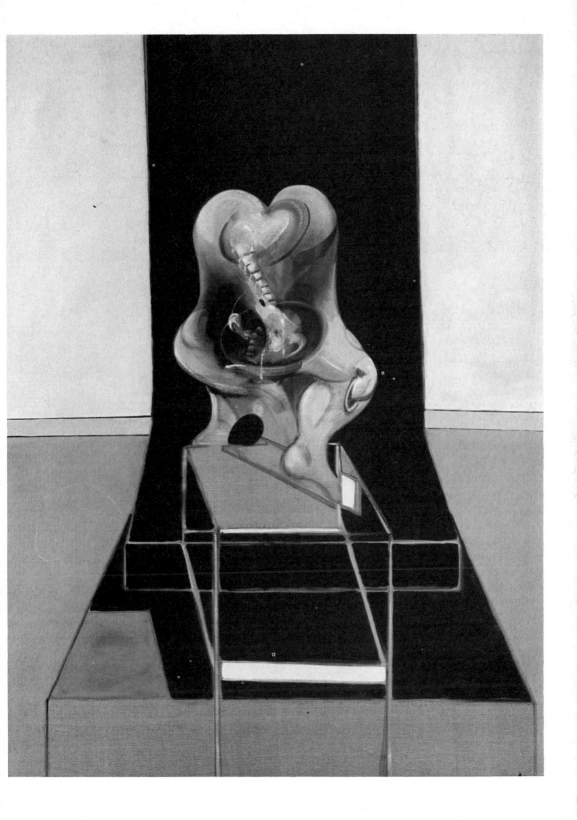

# 9

DS I'd like to question you about a number of factual matters. They mostly have to do with your methods of working, but to begin, I'd like to try and clarify how your early life was divided between Ireland and England.

FB Well, I was born in Ireland, though my mother and father were both English. My father was a trainer of racehorses and we lived near the Curragh, where more or less all the trainers were concentrated. I was born in Dublin but that was in a nursing home: the place where we lived was a house called Canny Court, near a small town called Kilcullen in County Kildare. We were there until the beginning of the First World War, when I was not quite five. My father went into the War Office and we came to live in London, in Westbourne Terrace. I remember that when there was a blackout they used to spray the Park with something phosphorescent out of watering cans thinking that the Zeppelins would suppose it was the lights of London and drop the bombs on the Park; it didn't work at all. So I was here for a time during the war. And then we vacillated very much between England and Ireland. Immediately after the war my father bought a house called Farmleigh in Abbeyleix in the county of Leix. He bought it from my grandmother – my mother's mother. She was an eccentric woman, one could say, and she was forever changing houses. She had a very curious relationship with my father: I think he disliked her very much but nevertheless they were always exchanging houses. Farmleigh was a beautiful house where the rooms at the back were all curved: I suppose one never knows about those things, but perhaps this may be one of the reasons why I have often used curved backgrounds in triptychs. Well, then we drifted from one house to another. For some reason

140 (Opposite) Centre panel of *141*

**184**

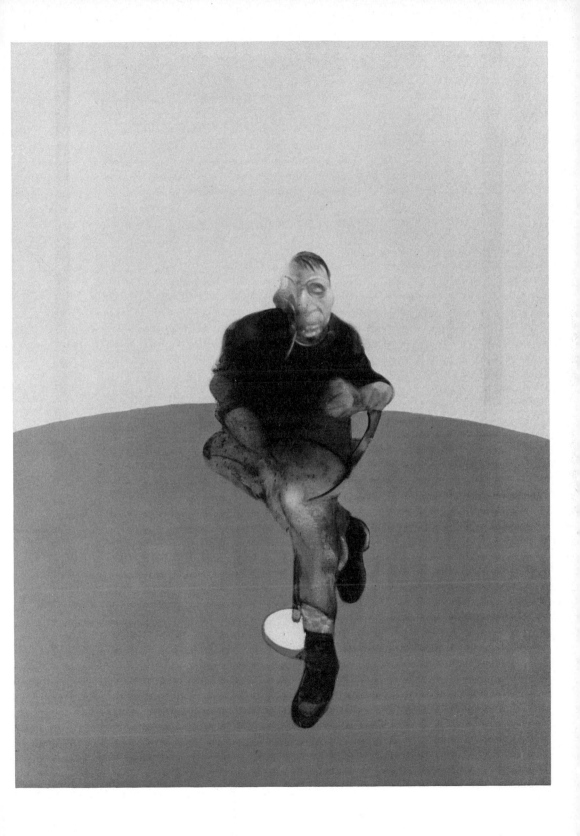

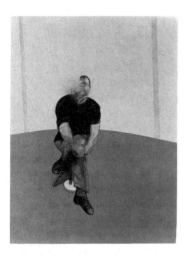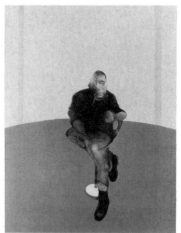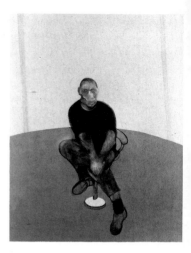

141 *Study for Self-Portrait – Triptych* 1985–6

my father and mother were never satisfied with where they were. So they moved back to England – to somewhere called Linton Hall, on the borders of Gloucestershire and Herefordshire. That didn't last very long, and they went back to Ireland, to a place called Straffan Lodge which was near Naas.

DS   Where did you go to school? Or did you not?

FB   I went for a short time to a place called Dean Close, in Cheltenham. It was a kind of minor public school and I didn't like it. I was continually running away, so in the end they took me away. I was there only about a year. So I had a very limited education. Then, when I was about sixteen, my mother made me an allowance. She had a bit of money of her own; she came from Firth's steel – I expect you've seen the name on knives. She made me an allowance of £3 a week, which in those days was enough to exist on. I came to London, and then I went to Berlin. One is always helped when one is young because people always like you when you are young, and I went with somebody who had picked me up – or whatever you like to say – to stay at the Adlon Hotel. It was the most wonderful hotel. I always remember the wheeling-in of the breakfast in the morning – wonderful trolleys with enormous swans' necks coming out of the four corners. And then the night life of Berlin was very exciting for me, coming straight from Ireland. But I didn't stay in Berlin very long. I went to Paris then for a short time. While there I saw at Rosenberg's an exhibition of Picasso, and at that moment I thought, well I will try and paint too.

142 (Opposite) Left-hand panel of *141*

**186**

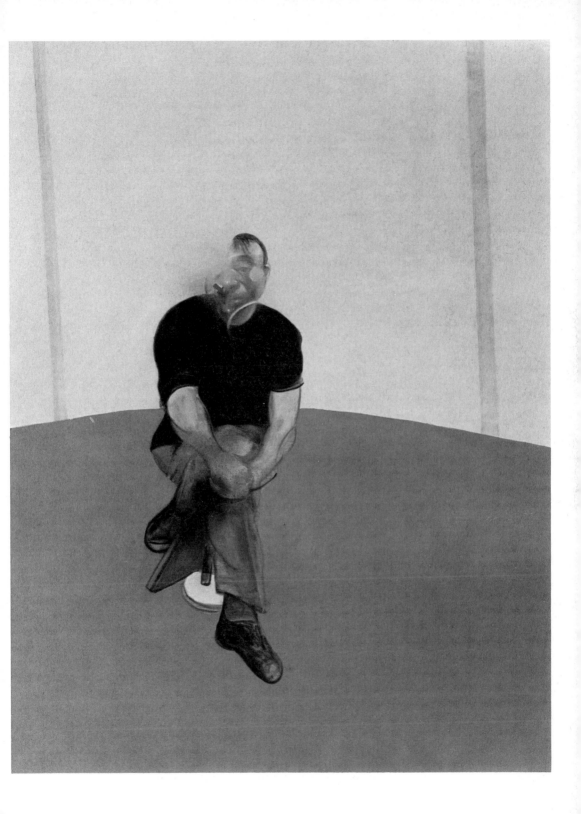

DS   How did your parents react when they heard about that idea?

FB   Well, my relationship with my father and mother was never good. We never got on. They were horrified at the thought that I might want to be an artist. They said, well, you will never earn your living as an artist, there is no possible chance of it, so they were totally against it. I can't say I had a happy home life. I had two brothers and two sisters, but one of my brothers went out to Rhodesia and joined the Rhodesian Police and was sent out when the Zambezi was in flood and was taken ill and somehow he got tetanus and died. And my younger brother died very early on. I remember the only time that I ever saw my father show any emotion was when my younger brother died; he was really very very fond of my younger brother. But I had no real relationship at all with my father. He didn't like me and he didn't like the idea that I was going to be an artist. You see, there was no tradition of that kind in the family at all, and they thought it was just an eccentricity in a son of theirs to think that he would like to be an artist. And it's true to say that it was years before I started painting regularly. I had all sorts of odd jobs. I tried to learn a form of shorthand which was called speed-writing; well, of course, I invented my own sort of speed writing. I was in various offices doing odd jobs and I was in a wholesale shop in Poland Street where I had to just answer the telephone and that was about all. I had a job for about six or eight months as a servant. I was a cook to somebody in Mecklenburgh Square, and a general servant. I had to arrive there at seven o'clock in the morning to get what is called the boss's breakfast. I can't say that I did a lot of housework. I turned the bed over and left very early. I used to have to go back at seven o'clock in the evening to cook a bit of dinner for him. He was a solicitor somewhere, I can't remember where. I always remember that when I gave in my notice he said to someone, 'I can't think why he's leaving because he doesn't do anything.' I was quite a good cook because my mother was an extremely good cook and so I just learned how to cook moderately well. Those were some of my jobs. When the war started I was turned down from the Army because I was an asthmatic: it's in my family and I have always been an asthmatic. I was turned down, I think, because they thought that they would have to pay me a pension for the rest of my life. I was put into the reserve service of the ARP, but I had such bad asthma that I was turned out of that. So then I was on my own. And it was then, about 1943–44, that I really started to paint. Nothing had really coagulated until then.

DS  I think that was shortly after you moved into the studio which you still had when we first met in 1950, the studio in Millais's old house in Cromwell Place.

FB  That was a wonderful studio. But, you know, when the war started and the bombs came, the whole of the roof of Millais's studio had been blown in, and the room I painted in was never built as a studio. It was an enormous billiard room, like the Edwardians often used to have at the backs of their houses. But it was a wonderful studio. I just had to get out of it because of many things – someone I was very fond of died there and I just didn't want to stay there. I have got two regrets in my life. One is giving up that place and the other one is giving up the place in Narrow Street.

DS  That was a beautiful house, with that view over the river. I think I've always assumed that you didn't do any painting there.

FB  Well, I did try, but, as the Thames is tidal, when the tide was in and the sun was out, there was a continual glitter inside the place which made it extremely difficult to work in. Nevertheless, the East End is such a wonderful area of London that I very much regret I gave it up.

DS  I remember your also having trouble with the light when you were working in that large studio off the King's Road which Michael Astor lent you in the early 1950s after you'd given up Cromwell Place.

FB  I wasn't able to work there because, although it was a beautiful studio with a beautiful skylight, it had trees above it and they waved in the wind, so that in the studio the light moved and it was like attempting to paint a picture under water.

DS  I remember your various studios in the course of the 1950s, even one at Henley. But you've been in this present place for a very long time now, have you not?

FB  I think I came here in 1961, so I have been here more than twenty years. For some reason the moment I saw this place I knew that I could work here. I am very influenced by places – by the atmosphere of a room, you know. And I just knew from the very moment that I came here that I would be able to work here. And I felt the same thing about the place in Paris. It's only one room, but I knew from the moment I went into it that it was a place I could work in.

DS   But in fact you haven't worked in it as much as you had expected to.

FB   No, I haven't. I do find that because I know London better than Paris I'm able to work more easily than in a city which I don't know so well.

DS   How was it when you were in Tangier in the 1950s?

FB   I did paint a certain amount there but not at all successfully. It didn't seem to really work. I think perhaps the light was too strong. I have tried to work in a lot of places. At one time I tried in Monte Carlo but again I am not as used to light as strong as that and therefore it in a sense interfered with me.

DS   Was it the light in this studio that particularly made you like the place when you saw it?

FB   No. I had the ceiling taken off, so it isn't the same light, and the light is not especially good because it's east–west. But the place had an atmosphere that made me know I could work here. I can't explain why. There are certain places where you know you can work and there are certain places where you know you can't. It's very odd: I don't know how one can explain the atmosphere of places. I suppose it is the way a place is constructed. This one had a low ceiling like the one in the next room, but I had the ceiling taken off in here and the council allowed me to put in that small skylight.

DS   I know how attached you must be to this place. You've told me that when those canvases of yours are brought up and down the stairs and into and out of the room, there's only one inch to spare. So it can't be exactly convenient, yet you've stayed twenty years.

FB   I feel at home here in this chaos because chaos suggests images to me. And in any case I just love living in chaos. If I did have to leave and I went into a new room, in a week's time the thing would be in chaos. I do like things to be clean, I don't want the plates and things to be filthy dirty, but I like a chaotic atmosphere.

DS   It's probably easier to work in a space that's chaotic. If painting or writing is an attempt to bring order to the chaos of life, and the room you're working in is disordered, I think it may act unconsciously as a spur to create order. Whereas, if you try to do it in a very tidy room, there seems to be much less point in getting started.

FB  Yes, I absolutely agree with you. I once bought a beautiful studio round the corner in Roland Gardens, with the most perfect light, and I did it up so well, with carpets and curtains and everything, that I absolutely couldn't work in it, and I gave it to a friend of mine. I made it too grand. I was absolutely castrated in the place. That was because I had done it up so well and I hadn't got the chaos. Another thing about chaos is that I can use the dust. I used dust from the studio in doing those paintings of the sand dunes that I

143 *Sand Dune* 1983

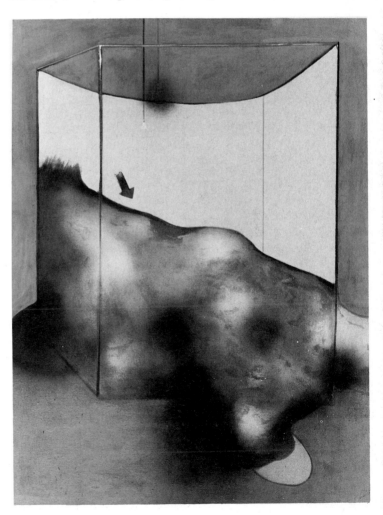

saw in Brittany. It's an awful game getting all that dust up from the floor but there is plenty of it here, as you know, stuck to pictures and everything else. So I just took dust and a cloth and put it onto the wet paint and after it was dried I set it as one sets a pastel. And that early painting in the Tate Gallery of Eric Hall in which his suit looks immaculate is painted with dust. Actually there is no paint at all on the suit apart from a very thin grey wash on which I put dust from the floor. Well, dust seems to be eternal – seems to be the one thing that lasts for ever – and one of the things that I have noticed and been very pleased to see is that it doesn't seem to have changed at all; it seems to be as fresh as when I first put it on forty years ago. The only trouble with the dust I have here now is that I have been using pastel so that a lot of the dust has become coloured. But pure dust is the perfect colour for a grey suit. It's a kind of pastel, really, but probably more lasting than pastel. I don't know, perhaps not more lasting, I don't know about the lastingness of things. But that is how it was, because I thought: well, how can I make that slightly furry quality of a flannel suit? And then I suddenly thought: well, I'll get some dust. And you can see how near it is to a decent grey flannel suit.

DS   I must look up the Tate Gallery catalogue and see if the description of the medium is correct.

FB   Well, of course they wouldn't like it suggested. They probably think it's pastel or something like that. But it's nothing but dust – whereas in the sand dune paintings dust is just incorporated in the colour to give it its texture.

DS   In talking about studios you've mentioned the light several times, so I take it that you do paint mainly by daylight.

FB   I nearly always paint by daylight, yes. When I was very young I used to work very much by night. But now I do work by daylight.

DS   Do you ever go on at night with a painting that you have been painting by daylight?

FB   I do sometimes, if I have got a certain distance with it and I think that it is going well. Then I just go on tinkering with it even at night.

DS   You start in the morning pretty early, don't you?

FB   I like starting very early, yes. I find that I am much

144 (Opposite) *Figure in a Landscape* 1945

**192**

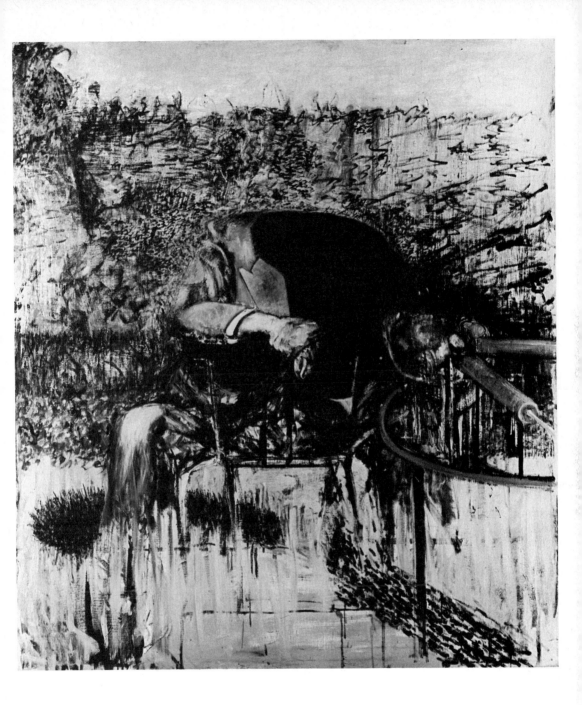

freer in the morning. Everything comes to me more easily then than later. I know many artists don't start till about noon and then go on through the afternoon and into the night, but I find that early in the morning works much better for me generally. If it works at all.

DS   Do you tend to find that you go on working for several hours without a break?

FB   If it's going well I can go on without a break, but sometimes when I think that it's going well I do stop, because, if I have a break of ten minutes, I can have forgotten what I had been doing and can come back and see it again clearly.

DS   You've often said that when you're painting you very much prefer to be alone – that, for instance, when you are doing a portrait you don't like to have the subject actually there.

FB   I feel that I am much freer if I'm on my own, but I'm sure that there are a lot of painters who would perhaps be even more inventive if they had people round them. It doesn't happen in my case. I find that if I am on my own I can allow the paint to dictate to me. So the images that I'm putting down on the canvas dictate the thing to me and it gradually builds up and comes along. That is the reason I like being alone – left with my own despair of being able to do anything at all on the canvas.

DS   Do you ever have the radio on when you're painting?

FB   No. I used to have music on sometimes, but I'm not musical. Really I prefer just being alone here. In any case, I work in a kind of haze. I don't want the work to be hazy, but I work in a kind of haze of sensations and feelings and ideas that come to me and that I try to crystallize. And then when something comes up that I think will work for me I become more specific. I think that has to do with using your critical faculty – where you suddenly see an opening, where you see the possibility of an image arising which you hadn't contemplated before.

DS   I suppose it's because you improvise so much that you're exceptional in doing figurative paintings as big as yours without any kind of preliminary drawing or oil sketch.

FB   Well, I sketch out very roughly on the canvas with a brush, just a vague outline of something, and then I go to work, generally using very large brushes, and I start painting immediately and then gradually it builds up.

DS   I presume you don't paint in those flat backgrounds until the figures are at a certain stage of realization.

FB   No, I generally put the background in at the end.

DS   That is completely different from when you were working thirty years ago with those backgrounds of very diluted dark blue or black paint. Then you used to put the ground on first and work on top of it.

FB   Yes, but then I used to put on very thin washes of colour. The paint was just mixed very thinly with turpentine and I put the whole wash on before I started putting the images down. But now I nearly always use acrylic paint for the backgrounds, and I don't want to work on the top of the acrylic because I like the absorption that the raw canvas has for the image.

DS   So you have continued to paint on unprimed canvas?

FB   Yes.

DS   But always with the other side primed?

FB   Yes.

DS   At what stage do you tend to put in the acrylic ground?

FB   When I feel that I have to some extent formed the image. I put the background in to see how it's going to work, and then I go on with the image itself.

DS   Do you often find that you have to change the original colour of the ground at some stage?

FB   I generally stay with the ground because it is extremely difficult to change it when you are using unprimed canvas. And also you have got to realize that a number of the backgrounds that I use on this unprimed canvas are pastel, because I find that with pastel you can get a much more intense colour and it holds very well on the unprimed canvas. It's like using very rough paper, like pastel paper. This thing of using unprimed canvas came about when I was living in Monte Carlo in the late 1940s. I had no money – probably I had lost it in the casino – but I had some canvases there which I had already used, so I turned them and discovered that the unprimed side was much easier to work on. And since then I have always worked on the unprimed side of the canvas.

DS   Obviously this is an impossible thing to generalize about, but how long does it tend to take you to paint a large triptych?

FB   I think about two or three weeks, but it can sometimes take two months.

DS   Do you nowadays still sometimes abandon a large painting when you have been working on it for a week or so?

FB   Well, if I have been working on it for some time and it just doesn't seem to be right, I cut it up and destroy it because the paint becomes so clogged and there is nothing to do, as I really do like paint to be very fresh.

DS   Sometimes you send a painting to Marlborough, get it back in the studio after a few days, and go on with it. Is it more usually a success or a mistake when you re-work it?

FB   It's true to say that I sometimes let paintings out too soon because I find that if they are in the studio I go on fiddling with them. But there is this other side, that I do know that very often, when I have had paintings back, it has helped me a great deal to see them again and I have been able to add to them. I think that it was Renoir who said that one should turn the canvas to the wall for three months and forget about what one was trying to do and then one will see the result without remembering what one had been trying to do.

DS   And you don't do that, do you?

FB   I don't do that, because the space I live in is too small. But I do agree that after about three months you have forgotten what you wanted to do and so you see it again raw.

DS   I can think of one painting which you were able to change very successfully even some years after it was done, which was a triptych of 1974 (*105–07*), the central panel of which had a reclining figure in the foreground which you painted out in 1977.

FB   I think it looks very much better without that thing in the foreground. I think I painted it out very well so that it couldn't come back. I hope you don't see it emerging again ever. I don't see it emerging in my lifetime, at least.

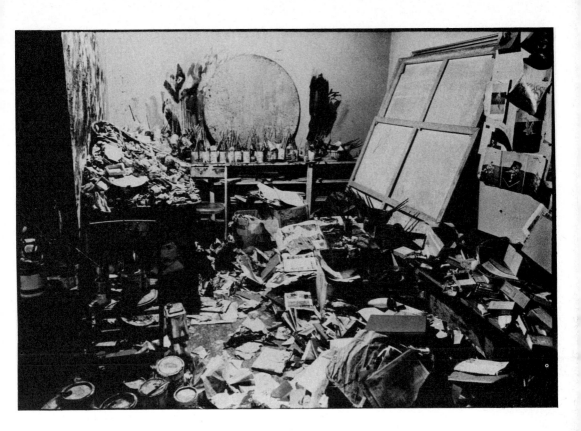

145 Bacon's studio

DS   Your titles: how do they come about?

FB   Well, I really try to use the most anonymous titles possible. So I nearly always call the things Studies for this or for that. And the Marlborough Gallery add the titles partly because they want to be able to remember what the pictures were. For one thing, they want to try and get these things for exhibitions or something like that, and it is easier if there is a title labelled onto them. For instance, with the painting that I did which the Marlborough called *Triptych – inspired by T.S. Eliot's poem 'Sweeney Agonistes'* (*103–04*), they had asked me how these images came about and I said that I had just been reading *Sweeney Agonistes* and they titled it in the way they did. And that is how those titles very often come about. But I really want to keep them as anonymous as possible, because I think that the titles lie within the images and people can read what they like into them.

DS   You do like to leave the spectator free to read the work as he sees it. But don't the crasser misinterpretations sometimes irritate you very much?

FB   They don't irritate me because I understand that that is how things are. I mean people can interpret things as they want. I don't even interpret very much what I do. By saying that, don't think that I think that I'm inspired, but I work and what I do I may like the look of, but I don't try to interpret it. After all, I'm not really trying to *say* anything, I'm trying to *do* something. Also, when I started to paint, I never expected anybody to ever buy my work. I did it to excite myself, and I always thought that I would have to do some other kind of job to earn my living. So that, though I have gradually been lucky enough to sell paintings and been able to live by my work, I think that I still have the same indifference to what other people think about it.

DS   You really are not working with any thought of an audience?

FB   I'm working for myself; what else have I got to work for? How can you work for an audience? What do you imagine that an audience would want? I have got nobody to excite except myself, so I am always surprised if anybody else likes my work sometimes. I suppose I'm very lucky, of course, to be able to earn my living by something that really absorbs me to try and do, if that is what you call luck.

DS   And your position is such that, of course, you hardly ever do a portrait on request.

FB   Not very often. Because most people want to be flattered by their portraits. It's a very odd thing about portraiture that people have an inbuilt idea of what they look like or what they want to look like. If you deviate from that, they don't like it. Also, I like doing portraits of people that I like – that I like as people and I like the look of. I would find it very difficult to do people that I really disliked. I suppose I could do caricatures of them – even more caricatural than I do in the ordinary way.

DS   Anyway, you don't have to. And it seems that the circumstances in which the artist works today suit you very well. You paint what you like to paint and your work goes to your gallery.

FB   That does suit me very well indeed, yes. My gallery don't bother me. I just work in isolation and when I have done something which I want to let go, they come and collect it. And they may sell it and they may not.

DS  That is to say, the whole set-up of society today suits you and your attitude towards work?

FB  I want my life to be as free as possible, I just want the best kind of atmosphere to work in. And so in politics I have tended to vote for the Right because they are less idealistic than the Left and therefore one is left freer than one would be if encumbered by the idealism of the Left. I always feel that for me the Right is the best of a bad job.

DS  What do you think are the essential things that go to make an artist, especially now?

FB  Well, I think that there are lots of things. I think that one of the things is that, if you are going to decide to be a painter, you have got to decide that you are not going to be afraid of making a fool of yourself. I think another thing is to be able to find subjects which really absorb you to try and do. I feel that without a subject you automatically go back into decoration because you haven't got the subject which is always eating into you to bring it back – and the greatest art always returns you to the vulnerability of the human situation. And then too, to be a painter now, I think that you have to know, even if only in a rudimentary way, the history of art from pre-historic times right up to today. You see, I have looked at everything in art. And also at many kinds of documentary books. I have looked at books of wild animals, for instance, because those images excite me and every so often one of them may come up to me and suggest some way to use the human body; and there was a book that I bought years and years ago somewhere of images of filters – they were just filters of different kinds of liquids, but the way they were formed suggested all sorts of ways in which I could use the human body (after all, the human body is in a sense a filter, apart from its other attributes). And I have also looked a great deal at the cinema. I was certainly, when I was much younger, influenced by the films of Eisenstein, and then after that I was also very influenced by the films of Buñuel, especially the early ones, because I think that he too had a remarkable precision of imagery. I can't say how they directly affected me but they certainly have affected my whole attitude to visual things – by showing the acuteness of the visual image that you have got to make.

DS  Have you come across a remark of André Bazin's that

Buñuel's cruelty was a means to rediscover humanity in all its grandeur?

FB    Is it real cruelty in Buñuel? Anything in art seems cruel because reality is cruel. Perhaps that's why so many people like abstraction in art, because you can't be cruel in abstraction.

DS    You think that people like abstract art for having anodyne qualities? You think they like it because 'human kind cannot bear very much reality', as Eliot puts it?

FB    Yes. I suppose he joined the church because he wanted an anodyne.

DS    Well, I don't know that the doctrines of the church are terribly anodyne. The idea of man's being redeemed only through the crucifixion of God's only son seems a fairly tragic view of life. And then there may be the carrot of beatitude but there's also the threat of hell. Don't you think that any believing Christian who felt that he was damned would prefer not to have an immortal soul than to live in eternal torment?

FB    No, I don't. I think that people are so attached to their egos that they'd probably rather have the torment than simple annihilation.

DS    You'd prefer the torment yourself?

FB    Yes, I would, because, if I was in hell I would always feel I had a chance of escaping. I'd always be sure that I'd be able to escape. □ □ □

146 (Opposite) *Study for Self-Portrait* 1982

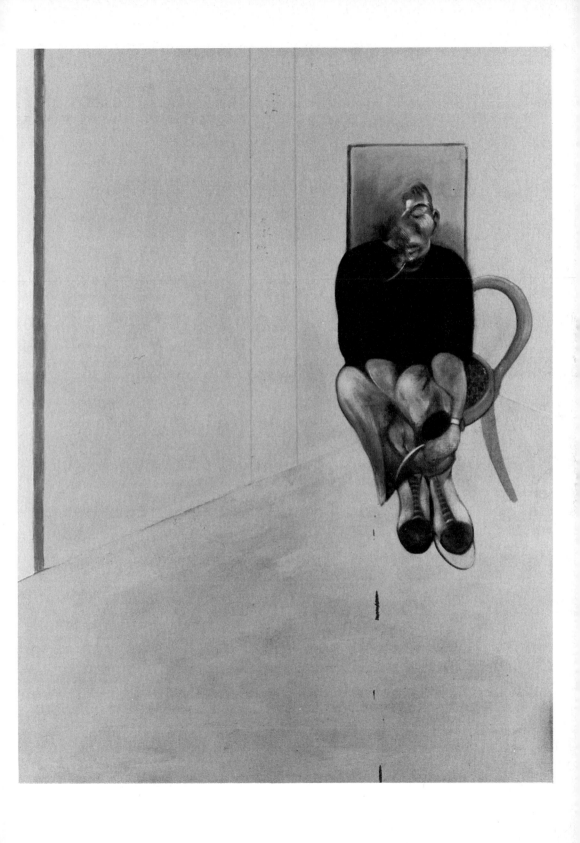

# Editorial Note

The interviews have been constructed by cutting and rearranging transcripts of tape recordings. Each interview is derived, with one exception, from two or more recordings: these were made on consecutive days in one case, but in every other case time elapsed between them. Extracts from the various recordings used for an interview are freely interwoven, sometimes even within a sentence. There is no correspondence between any particular section of an interview and any particular recording, nor are the breaks between the sections intended to indicate a passing of time, since each interview represents a single notional meeting.

Interview 1
dates from 1962.

It is based on a recording made by the BBC in October 1962. A version for radio, produced by Leonie Cohn, 'Francis Bacon talking to David Sylvester', was first broadcast on 23 March 1963. A version for publication, 'The Art of the Impossible', first appeared in *The Sunday Times Colour Magazine* on 14 July 1963.

Interview 2
dates from 1966.

It is based on three days of filming by the BBC in May 1966. A version for television was embodied in a film, written and directed by Michael Gill, *Francis Bacon: Fragments of a Portrait*, first transmitted on 18 September 1966. A version for publication, 'From Interviews with Francis Bacon by David Sylvester', first appered in *Francis Bacon: Recent Paintings*, the catalogue of an exhibition at Marlborough Fine Art, London, in March-April 1967.

Interview 3
dates from 1971–73.

It is based on three private recordings made in December 1971, July 1973 and October 1973.

Interview 4
dates from 1974.

It is based on two private recordings made in September 1974.

Interview 5
dates from 1975.

It is based on a videotape recording made by London Weekend Television in April 1975 and a private recording made in June 1975. A version of the former, produced by Derek Bailey, was transmitted in *Aquarius* on 30 November 1975.

Interviews 6 and 7
date from 1979.

Both are based on three private recordings made in March, August and September 1979.

Interview 8
dates from 1982–84.

It is mainly based on a recording made by Lecon Arts in March 1982, produced by Leonie Cohn. A version was issued as one of a series of cassettes with slides, *Artists Talking*, in 1985. A version for publication, 'Francis Bacon and David Sylvester: An unpublished interview', appeared in *Francis Bacon: peintures récentes*, the catalogue of an exhibition at the Galerie Maeght Lelong, Paris, in January-February 1984. That text is supplemented here, firstly, by the insertion of remarks remembered from conversation (and confirmed by Bacon), and secondly, by passages derived from the transcripts of recordings made on three days in March 1984 for a film directed by Michael Blackwood, *The Brutality of Fact*, first screened by BBC Television on 16 November 1984. A few short passages edited from those transcripts were included in 'Artist's dialogue: Francis Bacon' in *Architectural Digest*, Los Angeles, June 1985, pp. 90 and 94.

Interview 9
dates from 1984–86.

It is almost entirely based on the transcripts, also used for Interview 8, of the recordings made for the film, *The Brutality of Fact*, in March 1984. For the rest, it is derived from notes made after conversations in 1985–86. It has appeared as 'An unpublished interview by David Sylvester' in *Francis Bacon: Paintings of the Eighties*, the catalogue of an exhibition at the Marlborough Gallery, New York, in May-July 1987.

# Acknowledgments

Shena Mackay gave help with the editing for which I am much indebted. Her acuity found solutions to many of the more intractable problems.

Hugh Davies, Andrew Forge and Christopher White contributed expert advice on particular points.

Marlborough Fine Art have been endlessly patient providers of both photographs and information.

The staff of Thames and Hudson have been helpful critically, creatively and practically.

# List of Illustrations

*Photographs, unless otherwise credited, were provided by Marlborough Fine Art (London), Ltd. The measurements are given in inches and centimetres, height before width.*

**1** (Frontispiece) Detail of centre panel of *141*.

**2** Pablo Picasso: Untitled charcoal drawing, 1927. $13\frac{5}{8} \times 19\frac{7}{8}$ (34.5 × 50.5).

**3** *Three Studies for Figures at the Base of a Crucifixion*, 1944. Triptych, oil and pastel on hardboard, each 37 × 29 (94 × 74). Tate Gallery, London.

**4** Centre panel of *3*.

**5** Painting, 1946. Oil and tempera on canvas, $77\frac{7}{8} \times 52$ (198 × 132). Museum of Modern Art, New York.

**6** *Three Studies for Portrait of Henrietta Moraes*, 1963. Small triptych, oil on canvas, each 14 × 12 (35.5 × 30.5). Collection of Mr William S. Paley, New York.

**7** *Head I*, 1961. Oil on canvas $14\frac{3}{4} \times 12\frac{1}{4}$ (37.5 × 31). Private collection, London.

**8** *Three Studies for a Crucifixion*, 1962. Triptych, oil on canvas, each 78 × 57 (198 × 145). The Solomon R. Guggenheim Museum, New York.

**9** Cimabue: *Crucifixion* 1272–4 (inverted). Oil on wooden panel, $176\frac{3}{8} \times 153\frac{1}{2}$ (448 × 389.9). Chiesa di Santa Croce, Florence.

**10** Right-hand panel of *8*.

**11** *Study for Portrait of Van Gogh II*, 1957. Oil on canvas, 78 × 56 (198 × 142). Collection of Edwin Janss Jr., California.

**12** Van Gogh: *The Painter on his Way to Work* or *The Road to Tarascon*, 1888. Formerly in the Kaiser-Friedrich Museum, Magdeburg. Destroyed during the war.

**13** *Head II*, 1949. Oil on canvas, $31\frac{3}{4} \times 25\frac{5}{8}$ (80.5 × 65). Ulster Museum, Belfast.

**14** *Pope I*, 1951. Oil on canvas, 78 × 54 (198 × 137). Aberdeen Art Gallery and Industrial Museum.

**15** *Pope II*, 1951. Oil on canvas, 78 × 54 (198 × 137). Kunsthalle, Mannheim.

**16** *Pope III*, 1951. Oil on canvas, 78 × 54 (198 × 137). Destroyed by the artist in 1966.

**17** *Study for Portrait*, 1949. Oil on canvas, $58 \times 51\frac{1}{2}$ (147.5 × 131). Collection of Mr and Mrs Joseph R. Shapiro, Illinois.

**18** Velasquez: *Pope Innocent X*, 1650. Oil on canvas, $55\frac{1}{8} \times 47\frac{1}{4}$ (140 × 120). Galleria Doria Pamphili, Rome.

**19** *Pope*, 1954. Oil on canvas, $60 \times 45\frac{7}{8}$ (152.5 × 116.6). Private collection, Switzerland.

**20** *Study of Red Pope (Study from Innocent X)*, 1962. Oil on canvas, 78 × 57 (198 × 145). Collection of Mr M. Riklis, New York.

21 *Study for a Head*, 1955. Oil on canvas, 40 × 30 (101.5 × 76). Private collection, France.

22 *Study after Velasquez's Portrait of Pope Innocent X*, 1953. Oil on canvas, 60¼ × 46½ (153 × 118). Des Moines Art Center, Iowa.

23 *Study after Velasquez*, 1950. Oil on canvas, 78 × 54 (198 × 137). Destroyed by the artist in 1951.

24 Centre panel of *25*.

25 *Study for Three Heads*, 1962. Small triptych, oil on canvas, each 14 × 12 (35.5 × 30.5). Collection of Mr William S. Paley, New York.

26 *Study for Portrait III (after the life mask of William Blake)*, 1955. Oil on canvas, 24 × 20 (61 × 51). Private collection.

27, 28 Eadweard Muybridge: Sequence of photographs from *The Human Figure in Motion*, 1887.

29 Series of photographs from K. C. Clark, *Positioning in Radiography*, London, 1939 (not as caption).

30 Photograph from *Positioning in Radiography*.

31 Eadweard Muybridge: Page of selected photographs in some editions of *The Human Figure in Motion*.

32 Marius Maxwell: Photograph from *Stalking Big Game with a Camera in Equatorial Africa*, London, 1924.

33 Sergei Eisenstein: Still from *The Battleship Potemkin*, 1925.

34 Nicholas Poussin: Detail from *The Massacre of the Innocents*, 1630–31 (with angle altered). Oil on canvas, 57⅞ × 67¾ (147 × 171.1). Museé Condé, Chantilly (Photo: Giraudon).

35 *Study from Portrait of Pope Innocent X*, 1965. Oil on canvas, 78 × 58 (198 × 147.5). Private collection.

36 John Deakin: Photograph of George Dyer.

37 John Deakin: Photograph of Isabel Rawsthorne.

38 John Deakin: Photograph of Lucian Freud.

39 John Deakin: Photograph of Henrietta Moraes.

40 Photographs of Bacon taken by himself in automatic booths. (Copyright Francis Bacon).

41 *Crucifixion*, 1965. Triptych, oil on canvas, each 78 × 58 (198 × 147.5). Bayerische Staatsgemäldesammlungen, Münich.

42 *Fragment of a Crucifixion*, 1950. Oil and cotton wool on canvas, 55 × 42¾ (140 × 108.5). Stedelijk Van Abbemuseum, Eindhoven.

43 Centre panel of *41*.

44 Edgar Degas: *After the Bath: Woman Drying Herself*, 1903. Pastel, 27½ × 28¾ (69.9 × 73). National Gallery, London.

45 *Study for Figure IV*, 1956–7. Oil on canvas, 60 × 46 (152.5 × 117). National Gallery of South Australia, Adelaide.

46 *Head VI*, 1949. Oil on canvas, 36¾ × 30¼ (93 × 77). Arts Council of Great Britain.

47 *Three Studies for Portrait of Lucian Freud*, 1965. Small triptych, oil on canvas, each 14 × 12 (35.5 × 30.5). Private collection, London.

48 *Three Figures in a Room*, 1964. Oil on canvas, each 78 × 58 (198 × 147.5). Musée National d'Art Moderne, Centre Georges Pompidou, Beaubourg, Paris.

49 Left-hand panel of *48*.

50 Detail from centre panel of *48*.

51 Rembrandt: *Self-Portrait*, c. 1659. Oil on canvas, 11¾ × 9¾ (30 × 24). Musée, Aix-en-Provence. The authenticity has recently been questioned by certain scholars.

52 Henri Michaux: Untitled ink drawing, 1962. 29 × 42 (73.7 × 106.7). Formerly in the collection of Francis Bacon.

53 Landscape, 1952. Oil on canvas, 55 × 42¾ (139.5 × 108.5). Private collection, Rome.

54 Detail from right-hand panel of *41*.

55 Furniture and rugs designed by Bacon, photographed in his studio, 1930. From a feature in *Studio*, 'The 1930 Look in British Decoration', August 1930.

**56** *Crucifixion,* 1933. Oil on canvas, $24\frac{3}{4} \times 19$ ($61 \times 48.5$). Trustees of Sir Colin and Lady Anderson, Jersey, C. I.

**57** *Man Drinking (Portrait of David Sylvester),* 1955. Oil on canvas, $24 \times 20$ ($61 \times 51$). Private collection, Paris.

**58** *Study for a Portrait,* 1953. Oil on canvas, $60 \times 46\frac{1}{2}$ ($152.5 \times 118$). Kunsthalle, Hamburg.

**59** *Two Figures,* 1953. Oil on canvas, $60 \times 45\frac{7}{8}$ ($152.5 \times 116.5$). Private collection, England.

**60** *Two Figures in the Grass,* 1954. Oil on canvas, $59\frac{3}{4} \times 46$ ($152 \times 117$). Private collection, Paris.

**61** *Triptych – August 1972.* Oil on canvas, each $78 \times 58$ ($198 \times 147.5$). Tate Gallery, London.

**62** Centre panel of *61.*

**63** *Lying figure with Hypodermic Syringe,* 1963. Oil on canvas, $78 \times 57$ ($198 \times 145$). University Art Museum, Berkeley, California.

**64** Velasquez: *Prince Philip Prosper,* 1659. Oil on canvas, $50\frac{3}{8} \times 39$ ($128 \times 99$). Kunsthistorisches Museum, Vienna.

**65** Edvard Munch: *The Scream,* 1893. Oil, pastel and casein on cardboard, $35\frac{7}{8} \times 28\frac{7}{8}$ ($91 \times 73.5$). National Gallery, Oslo.

**66** Henri Fuseli: *Ariadne Watching the Struggle of Theseus with the Minotaur,* c. 1815. Brown wash and white body colour, $24 \times 19\frac{3}{4}$ ($61 \times 50.2$). Collection of Mr and Mrs Paul Mellon, Upperville, Virginia.

**67** Alberto Giacometti: *Head of Diego,* 1955. Painted bronze, height $22\frac{1}{4}$ ($56.6$). (*Photo:* Claude Gaspari, copyright Fondation Maeght, France).

**68** *Three Studies of the Human Head,* 1953. Triptych, oil on canvas, each $24 \times 20$ ($61 \times 51$). Private collection.

**69** Detail from right-hand panel of *68.*

**70** *Three Studies of Isabel Rawsthorne (on light ground),* 1965. Small tryptych, oil on canvas, each $14 \times 12$ ($35.5 \times 30.5$). Private collection, London.

**71** Marcel Duchamp: *Three Standard Stoppages,* 1913–14. Three threads glued upon three glass panels, each $49\frac{3}{8} \times 7\frac{1}{4}$ ($125.4 \times 18.4$); inscribed on reverse: 'Un mètre de fil droit, horizontal. tombé d'un mètre de haut. 3 stoppages étalon; appartenant à Marcel Duchamp. 1913–14.' Three flat wooden strips repeating the curves of the threads, averaging 45 ($114.3$) in length. The Museum of Modern Art, New York, Katherine S. Dreier Bequest.

**72** *Portrait of George Dyer in a Mirror,* 1968. Oil on canvas, $78 \times 58$ ($198 \times 147.5$). Private collection, Switzerland.

**73** *Tryptich – May–June 1973.* Oil on canvas, each $78 \times 58$ ($198 \times 147.5$). Private collection, New York.

**74** Right-hand panel of *93.*

**75** Detail from right-hand panel of *91.*

**76** Pablo Picasso: *Houses on a Hill (Horta de San Juan),* 1909. Oil on canvas, $25\frac{1}{2} \times 32\frac{1}{4}$ ($65 \times 81.5$). Private collection, Paris.

**77** Pablo Picasso: *Still Life with a Violin,* 1911–12. Oil on canvas, $39\frac{1}{4} \times 28\frac{3}{4}$ ($100 \times 73$). Rijksmuseum Kröller-Müller, Otterlo.

**78** *Sleeping Figure,* 1974. Oil on canvas, $78 \times 58$ ($198 \times 147.5$). Collection of the artist.

**79** *Triptych – Studies from the Human Body,* 1970. Oil on canvas, each $78 \times 58$ ($198 \times 147.5$). M. Knoedler & Co., New York.

**80** Centre panel of *79.*

**81** *Study of Nude with Figure in a Mirror,* 1969. Oil on canvas, $78 \times 58$ ($198 \times 147.5$). Veranneman Foundation, Kruishouten.

**82** *Lying Figure in a Mirror,* 1971. Oil on canvas, $78 \times 58$ ($198 \times 147.5$). Marlborough Gallery Inc., New York.

**83** *Study for Crouching Nude,* 1952. Oil on canvas, $78 \times 54$ ($198 \times 137$). The Detroit Institute of Arts.

**84** *After Muybridge – Woman Emptying Bowl of Water and Paralytic Child on All Fours,* 1965. Oil on canvas, $78 \times 58$ ($198 \times 147.5$). Stedelijk Museum, Amsterdam.

85  *Seated Figure*, 1974. Oil and pastel on canvas, 78 × 58 (198 × 147.5). Private collection, Switzerland.

86  *Painting*, 1950. Oil on canvas, 78 × 52 (198.1 × 132.1). City Art Gallery, Leeds.

87  Michelangelo: Study for a putto and for the right hand of the Libyan Sibyl; sketches for the tomb of Julius II, 1511 and 1513. Red chalk, pen, $11\frac{1}{4} \times 7\frac{5}{8}$  (28.6 × 19.4).  Ashmolean Museum, Oxford. (*Photo:* Museum).

88  *Three Studies of Figures on Beds*, 1972. Triptych, oil and pastel on canvas, each 78 × 58 (198 × 147.5). Private collection.

89  Eadweard Muybridge: Photograph from *The Human Figure in Motion*, 1887.

90  Centre panel of *88*.

91  *Three Studies of the Male Back*, 1970. Triptych, oil on canvas, each 78 × 58  (198 × 147.5). Marlborough International.

92  Left-hand panel of *91*.

93  *Triptych – March 1974*. Oil on canvas,  each  78 × 58  (198 × 147.5). Private collection.

94  Centre Panel of *93*.

95  Left-hand panel of *61*.

96  *Portrait of Isabel Rawsthorne Standing in a Street in Soho*, 1967. Oil on canvas, 78 × 58 (198 × 147.5). Nationalgalerie, Berlin.

97  *Three Studies of a Portrait*, 1975. Small triptych, oil on canvas, each 14 × 12 (35.5 × 30.5). Private collection, Paris.

98  *Two Studies for Self-Portrait*, 1972. Small diptych, oil on canvas, each 14 × 12 (35.5 × 30.5). Private collection, Madrid.

99  *Portrait of a Dwarf*, 1975. Oil on canvas,  $62\frac{1}{2} \times 23$  (158.5 × 58.5). Private collection, Sydney.

100  *Self-Portrait*, 1972. Oil on canvas, 14 × 12 (35.5 × 30.5). Private collection, Switzerland.

101  *Three Studies for a Self-Portrait*, 1974. Small triptych, oil on canvas,  each  14 × 12  (35.,5 × 30.5). Collection of Mr and Mrs Carlos Haime, Bogotà.

102  *Self-Portrait*, 1973. Oil on canvas, 78 × 58 (198 × 147.5). Collection of Claude Bernard, Paris.

103  *Triptych – inspired by T. S. Eliot's poem 'Sweeney Agonistes'*, 1967.  Oil  on  canvas,  78 × 58 (198 × 147.5).  Hirshhorn Museum and Sculpture Garden, Washington, D.C.

104  Centre panel of *103*.

105  *Triptych 1974–77*. Oil and pastel  on  canvas,  each  78 × 58 (198 × 147.5). Collection of the artist.

106  Centre panel of *105*, first state, 1974.

107  Centre panel of *105*.

108  Left-hand panel of *105*.

109  *Three Studies for a Self-Portrait*, 1976. Small triptych, oil on canvas, each 14 × 12 (35.5 × 30.5). Private collection, Switzerland.

110  Left-hand panel of *109*.

111  *Three Studies for Self-Portrait*, 1979. Small triptych, oil on canvas, each $14\frac{3}{4} \times 12\frac{1}{2}$ (37.5 × 31.8). Marlborough International.

112  *Study of Henrietta Moraes*, 1969.  Oil  on  canvas,  14 × 12 (35.5 × 30.5). Private collection.

113  Right-hand panel of *111*.

114  *Portrait of Michel Leiris*, 1978. Oil on canvas, 14 × 12 (35.5 × 30.5). Collection of the artist.

115  *Portrait of Michel Leiris*, 1976. Oil on canvas, 14 × 12 (35.5 × 30.5). Collection of Michel Leiris, Paris.

116  *Painting 1978*. Oil on canvas, 78 × 58  (198 × 147.5).  Private collecton.

117  *Triptych 1971*. Oil on canvas, each  78 × 58  (198 × 147.5). Private collection, New York.

118  Centre panel of *117*.

119  Left-hand panel of *117*.

120  *Figure in movement*, 1976. Oil on canvas, 78 × 58 (198 × 147.5). Private collection, France.

121  *Triptych – Studies of the Human Body*, 1979. Oil on canvas, each 78 × 58  (198 × 147.5). Marlborough International.

**122**  Centre panel of *121*.

**123**  *Landscape*, 1978. Oil and pastel on canvas, 78 × 58 (198 × 147.5). Private collection, Switzerland.

**124**  First state of *123*.

**125**  *Jet of Water*, 1979. Oil on canvas, 78 × 58 (198 × 147.5). Marlborough International.

**126**  Right-hand panel of *127*.

**127**  *Triptych 1976*. Oil and pastel on canvas, each 78 × 58 (198 × 147.5). Private collection, France.

**128**  Centre panel of *127*.

**129**  *Figure in movement*, 1978. Oil and pastel on canvas, 78 × 58 (198 × 147.5). Private collection, Los Angeles.

**130**  Pablo Picasso: *Bather and Cabin*, Dinard, 9 August, 1928. Oil on canvas, $8\frac{1}{2} \times 6\frac{1}{4}$ (21.6 × 15.9). The Museum of Modern Art, New York. Hillman Periodicals Fund.

**131**  *Figure Writing Reflected in a Mirror*, 1976. Oil on canvas, 78 × 58 (198 × 147.5). Private collection.

**132**  *Study for a Portrait of John Edwards*, 1985. Oil on canvas, 78 × 58 (198 × 147.5). Marlborough International Fine Art.

**133**  *Study for Portrait of Gilbert de Botton*, 1986. Oil and pastel on canvas, 78 × 58 (198 × 147.5). Private collection.

**134**  *Study for Portrait of John Edwards*, 1986. Oil and pastel on canvas, 78 × 58 (198 × 147.5). Collection of the artist.

**135**  *A Piece of Waste Land*, 1982. Oil on canvas, 78 × 58 (198 × 147.5). Private collection.

**136**  *Triptych*, 1986–87. Oil and pastel on canvas, each 78 × 58 (198 × 147.5). Collection of the artist.

**137**  Centre panel of *136*.

**138**  *Triptych – inspired by the Oresteia of Aeschylus*, 1981. Oil on canvas, 78 × 58 (198 × 147.5). Marlborough International Fine Art.

**139**  Centre panel of *138*.

**140**  Centre panel of *141*.

**141**  *Study for Self-Portrait – Triptych*, 1985–86. Oil on canvas, each 78 × 58 (198 × 147.5). Marlborough International Fine Art.

**142**  Left-hand panel of *141*.

**143**  *Sand Dune*, 1983. Oil and pastel on canvas, 78 × 58 (198 × 147.5). Collection of Ernst Beyeler, Basle.

**144**  *Figure in a Landscape*, 1945. Oil on canvas, $57 \times 50\frac{1}{2}$ (145 × 128). Tate Gallery, London.

**145**  Peter Beard: Photograph of Bacon's studio.

**146**  *Study for Self-Portrait*, 1982. Oil on canvas, 78 × 58 (198 × 147.5). Private collection.